IN LOVE WITH MY 5 WIVES

BY
JAMES BASS

Published by

Clarice Jefferies Publishing

Contact info: cjpublishing@yahoo.com

Printed in United States of America on responsibly sourced paper.

Broken men break people, Broken people break people

I started this journey to help fix my broken wife. I helped break her. I broke her because I was broken. At the time, I did not know I was broke. I felt normal. I laughed. I joked. I had hobbies that I enjoyed. I had "friends." I had a career. Great pay. However, my life up to that point, had been very painful. To a broken person, with no self-love, no self-worth, and low self-esteem, pain became my best friend. I realized pain was the problem… pain. It was my normal. If there was no pain, then I would create pain so I could function "Normally." Do you see the irony? If there was no pain, then I would generate pain so I could feel normal. In doing so, I helped to further break someone that did not deserve to be hurt—my beautiful wife.

I was a cheater. I cheated on my wife (girlfriend/fiancé back then) multiple times. I was extremely abusive. I was abusive, verbally, emotionally, mentally, and physically. This abuse went on for 14 years. I'm going to let that sink in for a minute…14 years. From 1993 through 2007. That is a prison term that I sentenced my wife to serve. I was the judge, jury, and prosecutor. To me, this was normal. It was my life. I was, what I THOUGHT a man was supposed to be.

I had been broken without knowing I was broken. Better yet, broken is too cliché. I was a fucking mess. I was a pile of shit with shoes. I was shattered, and if I was shattered, then I had utterly obliterated my wife during this time.

Why was I this way? Who broke me? When was I broken? Who broke my wife? My wife was a broken woman before we met. I would not find out until 28yrs later how badly she had been damaged.

It is a vicious cycle. Most of us men are broken in some way, shape, or form. We were hurt by someone that was damaged by someone else. It is a cycle that only we, as men, have the power to stop. We can fix what we break and stop hurting others. But first. We have to do the most challenging thing of all…we have to heal and love ourselves. It is hard work. It is hard to fix someone else's fuck up's, but it needs to be done, especially when it comes to our mental health. Until you heal yourself, you can't mend broken relationships, and you can't help heal anyone else. With this book, I will do my best to explain.

For me, I was broken during my early childhood and teenage years. I was physically, mentally, and emotionally tormented, tortured, and abused. It lasted from 4 years old until I was 17. I had been torturously abused by my little brother's father, my little sister's father, and my mother.

SPECIAL THANKS AND RECOGNITION TO:

DR. MARCHITA MASTERS, CLINICAL PSYCHOLOGIST

DR. KELLY HORTON, CLINICAL PSYCHOLOGIST

DR. THOMAS ODEN, PSYCHIATRIST MD.

DR. MATTHEW TATUM, CLINICAL PSYCHOLOGIST / CEO,
SIERRA MEADOWS BEHAVIORAL HEALTH

EMILY GOMEZ, LMFT / CLINICAL DIRECTOR

DYLAN VANE, POST DOCTURNAL INTERN
/ STAFF CLINICIAN

BARBARA WOODWARD, NURSE PRACTITIONER

Each of you played a pivotal role in the support, rehabilitation, and restoration of my wife's emotional, psychological, and spiritual well-being and thus, adding to the quality of her life. Words shall never be enough to express my full gratitude.

To My Angelic Wife;

Mere words are insufficient as I search for a way to express my feelings,

I fear my vocabulary is not vast enough to capture the true essence of your resilience, benevolence, and companionship, and I fear I will diminish what you mean to me in an attempt to do so.

It is an absolute privilege to have met you,

An indescribable blissfulness when I hold you,

And an unfeigned honor to have become your husband.

As long as the night remains in the sky, my affection, my adoration, my every breath

Will remain, forever yours

TABLE OF CONTENTS

SID

I will start with my little brother's father. He is Mexican-American. We call him Sid. Sid used to beat and torture me. He would put his cigarette butts out on my shins. He would poke me up and down my back with thumbtacks, and water-torture me in the bathtub. He would beat me until I lost consciousness and then lock me up in a closet. I would wake up terrified in total darkness. He would turn up the music on the radio very loud to drown out my cries and screams. This went on for months. My mother, at the time, was attending college (As the story goes). The beatings would begin as soon as she walked out of the door. I remember, at times, crying uncontrollably, begging my mom not to leave. But she would leave me at his mercy. She had to go to school. The more I cried, the angrier Sid would become, and the more enraged he became, the worse the beating was.

I remember, on many occasions, when Sid would fill up the bathtub with water. He would make it a bubble bath. I would get in the tub to take a bath, and after a few minutes, Sid would come in, grab my ankles, and for some reason, pull me up in the air so that I would be upside down with my head below the water. I can remember, my body would go into spasms as a result of running short of oxygen. He would pull me up, just enough for me to gasp and choke for air and then he would lower me under again. Sid would repeat this process over and over. He would steep me in the bathtub like a teabag until I passed out. Then after that, he would lock me in the closet. This went on for many weeks, months, and years.

I remember the day my mother broke up with Sid. My mother fixed us fried chicken, macaroni & cheese, and green beans for dinner. (I hated green beans). As she finished washing dishes and was drying the skillet with a towel, there was a knock at the door, so my mom opened it. It was Sid. She kissed him and asked him how his day was. He began to explain his day as he turned his back to close the front door. As he turned around, our mother smashed him over his head with the skillet. She began to yell and cuss while beating him in the face with the frying pan. There was blood everywhere on his body.

She found out that Sid had been cheating on her with other women.

That is why I was locked in the closet. Whenever my mother left for school, Sid would bring other women over to the apartment. He could not have me tell what he was doing, so he would water torture me and then lock me in the closet. I wonder-who left Sid a broken man?

ROCK

◆━━━━━━━━━━━━━━◆

My little sister's father. We call him Rock. He is Mexican-American. Rock was a Vietnam veteran, a decorated Green Beret. A real hero to his country but a fucking asshole to me. He hated me. He loved to tell me how stupid I was. He would constantly call me a faggot and a pussy because of the way I dressed or styled my hair. Rock often referred to me as "Boy" and would regularly tell me how I would never amount to shit as I got older. His favorite catchphrase to tell me was, "No matter what you do, I will always have the last laugh." He had a lot of negative feelings toward me. I felt it was because he was ashamed to be seen out in public with me. You see, I'm mixed. I'm what you call a "Half-breed." My father was African-American. He died around 2011, and my mother is Mexican-American. My skin color is not the typical high yellow light skin that you see glorified on T.V- I am dark brown.

I remember countless times we would be out together as a "Family." Rock would tell me to get away from him or to go and walk somewhere else. I would have to walk separately from everyone, either a few feet in front of them, a few feet behind them, or off to the side. (As I got older,

I did this on my own by choice). I remember in elementary school; we had a Christmas assembly. My little brother's class was going to sing on stage. I saw Rock waiting outside the cafeteria. I was happy to see him, so I walked over to say hi and stand next to him. He shouted, "Get the hell away from me" as he walked away to stand somewhere else.

Rock used to have these flashbacks from the war. I remember on this one occasion; my little brother and I woke up in the middle of the night to our mother screaming. We got up and ran down the hallway. Rock dragged our mother out of bed, down the hall, and out onto the patio. We lived upstairs, and he had her by the neck, choking her. He had her back pushed against the rail and was trying to throw her over the balcony. He was shouting in Vietnamese. His eyes were closed. He was in the middle of a flashback. My mother was crying, screaming, trying to get away. My little brother and I just stood there helpless. Our mother finally dug her nails into his face waking him up.

These flashbacks would go on for years. I remember on another occasion (years later) when Rock chased us around the house with a machete. My brother and I locked ourselves in a bathroom that was located in my bedroom. He shoved the machete under the gap of the door and swung it side to side, trying to slash our feet. I jumped onto the sink, and my brother jumped onto the toilet. We could hear our mother screaming and crying for him to stop. She locked herself in the other bathroom. After several minutes, it was total silence. My brother and I thought our mother had been killed, so I frantically began to remove the screen from my bathroom window so that my brother and I could escape. About a minute later, we heard our mother say that everything had been okay, and we could come out. As we walked out of my bathroom, Rock just laughed it off as though it was some sort of joke. He gave no apologies.

I recall one occasion when I was terrified to bring my report card home. I was in 4th grade. It was another report card of mostly D's and F's. Rock warned me that if I ever brought home another report card like that, I would wish I was never born. So, I came up with the bright idea to tear up my report card, flush it down the toilet in the boy's bathroom, and tell my parents the teacher did not have mine.

I walked home after school. As soon as I walked through the door, my mother asked for my report card. I told her I did not get one. She yelled, "What do you mean, you did not get one?" I told her, "The teacher did not have mine." She got up from the kitchen table and grabbed the phone. She told me, "Don't you fucking move." She called the school and asked for my teacher. The office transferred my mother to the classroom, and my teacher confirmed that I received my report card. My mother hung up the phone and yelled, "You little fucking liar! Where the fuck is your report card!" Before I could answer, Rock came walking down the hallway from their bedroom and asked my mother why she was yelling. My mother told him what had taken place, and I began to panic, peeing in my pants. Rock grabbed me by the throat and shouted, "Boy, where is your report card!" I said, "In the trash can at school." My mother lunged at me and tried to slap me, but Rock had thrown me up against the front door. He stopped my mother and told her he would take care of it. He said, "We are going back to that school, and you are going to get that fucking report card." He opened the front door and kicked me outside. I got up from the cement floor, crying. We lived about 1 ½ blocks away from the school. As we were walking, Rock repeatedly slapped the back of my head and kicked the back of my legs for walking too slowly. "Hurry your ass up," he would yell with each kick.

We finally made it to the school. Rock yelled, "Now hurry the fuck up and get me that report card!" I ran frantically from trash can to trash can on the blacktop and playground looking into each one. The janitors must have picked up the trash because all the trash cans were empty. I just stood there as I finished looking into the last trash can. He yelled as he walked up to me, "What fucking trash can did you throw it in?" I told him, "The big one behind the cafeteria." He kicked me again and said, "Well, what the fuck are you looking out here for? Get your ass to that trash can and get that report card!"

I tried to run, but I couldn't. My legs were in too much pain from being kicked so many times. I hobbled to the big dumpster behind the cafeteria. I pointed at it and said, "I threw it in there." I hoped this would end the nightmare. I expected him to say, "Forget it let's go." Instead, he said, "Go in and get it." I just stood there crying. He kicked me in the chest, and I flew backward against the dumpster, banging the back of my head and splitting it open. I could remember screaming in pain as I held the back of my head, then looking at my hands and seeing blood. I could feel the blood run down the back of my neck as he shouted, "Get your ass in there and get that goddamn report card!" I got up and tried to climb in, but I could not. I was too small and too weak to pull myself up into the dumpster. As I tried again to pull myself up, Rock grabbed me hard by the top of my little afro, grabbed me between the legs, and threw me up and over face-first into the dumpster. It was full of cafeteria food, trash, and lawn clippings, and it smelled horrible. He yelled, "Hurry the fuck up!"

I peed on myself again, and vomited several times all over my pants and shoes because the stench from the trash was horrible. I was crying uncontrollably as I frantically searched for my report card. Finally, I stood up and told Rock, "It's not here." He said, "Bullshit, you're going to stay here until you fucking find it." I said, "No, it's not in the trash. I did not throw it away. I flushed it down the toilet." That came like a bomb blast to him. It was the last straw that broke the camel's back.

Rock stood there, staring at me. He was furious. I stumbled over the uneven trash to the edge of the dumpster and tried to pull myself out. He came over, grabbed me by the hair, and yanked me forward. My chest was pinned against the wall of the dumpster. He began slapping me back and forth across my face. He was yelling, "You stupid little fucking liar, you got me out here dealing with this bullshit!" He reached in and grabbed me by the back of my jeans and pulled me up and over, throwing me onto the blacktop, face first, busting my nose and my mouth. He yelled, "Get up and get your ass home!" I could barely manage to raise my frail body.

By then, I was bleeding from my nose, mouth, and the back of my head. My clothes were soaked with sweat, vomit, and pee, and I was being yelled at and kicked on our way home. As we walked through the front door, my mother looked over from the kitchen, saw the condition I was in, and asked Rock, "What the fuck happened?" He explained the situation I put him through as she walked over to me. I remember looking at her for help. My mother slapped the shit out of me as she yelled, "You little fucking liar!" Rock grabbed her and said, "I will handle this." He yelled, "Go to your room and pull down your pants."

I limped to my room, crying. I thought it had ended but Rock went ahead to the hallway closet and grabbed his leather belt. He came into my room and yelled, "I said pull down your pants." I pulled down my pants slowly. I was shaking uncontrollably. He said, "Pull down your underwear and turn around." I slowly pulled down my underwear, but I did not turn around. I did not want a beating. He yelled, "Turn around!" I just stood there, frozen. He snapped me back into reality by swinging the belt hard across the front of my legs, striking my penis in the process. I yelled as I covered my private area with both hands. He swung the belt striking me again. I tried to move away from him, but I had my pants and underwear pulled halfway down my legs. I couldn't move, I fell against my desk, he grabbed me by the shirt. He pulled me up and threw me face first against the wall next to my closet. He pinned me to the wall by pushing the left side of my face against the wall with one hand as he began to beat the shit out of me with the belt in his other hand. I remember yelling and screaming for help and yelling for him to stop. I was screaming out, "Stop! I'm sorry, I'm sorry!" The pain was excruciating. I peed on myself again. This time, from the combination of him smashing my head against the wall and the beating, I could feel myself losing consciousness. I reached up and grabbed his wrist and tried to pull his hand off the side of my head, but I was unsuccessful. The last images I remember seeing were the clouds outside of my bedroom window. I lost control of my body and began to poop on myself as I lost consciousness. Rock kept on swinging that damn belt.

I must have passed out for about a minute. When I finally regained consciousness, I found myself laying in a small puddle of poop, pee, and blood. Rock hit me so hard and so many times that he split open the back of my legs. I sat up and could see poop splattered everywhere. There was poop splattered on the walls, my bed, my desk, and the doors. My mother came to my bedroom door and set down a bucket of soapy water. She threw a sponge at me and yelled, "Take off your clothes and throw them in the trash. Open up your fucking window and clean this shit up." I could not even stand up. My legs were weak.

All of the kicks from the trip up to the school earlier and then the beating left me weak. I crawled around naked on my hands and knees and cleaned up the mess, the best I could.

About twenty minutes passed when the doorbell rang. It was my little sister's Godmother, Rock's sister, Sissy. I could hear my mom as she opened the door say, "Hey girl, what's up with you?" Sissy walked in and said, "Same old shit girl, you know." Then Sissy paused for a minute and asked, "Damn girl, what the fuck is that smell?" Rock answered, "It's J. J. (My childhood nickname). I guess you could say I beat the shit out of him. Ha ha ha!" I could hear him and my mother laughing but Sissy did not.

I missed almost a month of school as a result of this beating. I always missed a lot of school due to many beatings. I was also kept away from family members. I would be stuck in my bedroom for days and weeks at a time as I was being "healed" from my injuries, with Rock making sure I did not run away from home. I would cry in bed and stare at the ceiling, thinking about my Abuelita. I wanted to tell her what was going on, but my mom and Rock threatened me. I was told that if I ever said anything, I would have the life beaten out of me, and I would never see my Abuelita again. So, I just kept everything to myself. I wonder- who left Rock a broken man?

MY MOTHER

◆•──────────•──────────•◆

My mother is a prejudiced woman; she is Mexican-American. She had this hatred toward black men and women. When we passed by an average black man on the street, she would say to my little brother and me, "Look at that sorry ass nigger." If it were a black female, she would often refer to them as "Sorry ass worthless bitches and hoes." At first, my brother and I would laugh. We were little. We did not fully comprehend what was being said. We just heard an adult cussing. And to us, as children, it was funny. Besides, I was being raised in an all-Mexican-American family. I had no contact with any African American families or black culture.

I grew up in a predominantly Mexican-American neighborhood. My elementary school was the same. I remember the first time I was called a nigger at school. It was by two Mexican American boys, Andrew and Robert; they were brothers. They were playing tetherball. Everyone was out playing for recess. I went over and began to hit the ball in the middle of their game, just trying to play. The younger brother told me to stop, but I did not. I was having too much fun. His older brother grabbed the ball and said, "Get the fuck out of here nigger." They both began to laugh as I laughed with them. They stopped and looked at each other as if to ask, "What the hell are you laughing at?" Up to that point, I only heard my mother say nigger. It was funny because these kids were cursing using the same "Bad words" my mother used. It was not until I got into the 5th and 6th grade and began to "Learn history" that I started to understand the meaning of the word, nigger.

My mother was also a cheat. I remember her cheating on Sid, and Rock. In fact, my mother cheated on Sid with Rock. And Sid and Rock are brothers. So, that means my little brother and little sister are cousins. My mother's response to her actions is, "Well, at least I kept it in the family." My mother would often take my little brother and me along with her to visit "Mom's friends." I remember one of her friends, in particular; she "Visited" him a lot. His name was Jessie. He lived not too far from the apartment complex where we lived. I think he had a daughter about my age because the same little girl would be at his house when we visited. We would get to his house at the same time several days a week. I remember this because my little brother, this little girl, and I would sit in the living room for hours watching cartoons and the T.V that showed Wonder Woman, The Incredible Hulk, and The Six Million Dollar Man.

I look back as an adult and realize, that's three T.V shows, 30 min each show. That is 1 ½ hours total. It was no secret, that Jessie was "Visiting the shit" out of our mother. After visiting, on our way back home, my mother would tell us in Spanish, "Si papá te pregunta dónde estábamos, dile que estuvimos con la Abuela." My little brother did not speak or understand Spanish, so he would ask, "What mom, what did you say?" She would tell him, "If dad asks you where we were, just tell him we were at grandma's place."

I had trouble reading and writing in elementary school. I hated bringing assignments home. I was often beaten because my mother was easily frustrated if I did not understand as she tried to help me with my homework. I remember one incident; in particular, my mother had prepared meatloaf, mashed potatoes, and green beans for dinner. I just finished getting my ass beat for yet another failed homework lesson. I returned to the table and began to eat. My little brother was sitting across from me in his little yellow booster seat. As I ate, I began to gag on my green beans. My mother put butter on them. I hated butter on my green beans, and I hated green beans period! My mother yelled, "Stop fucking around and eat your food." I was still sobbing from the ass beating earlier, and now I began to choke and gag as I tried to eat these butter-drenched green beans. My gag reflex became more extreme with each mouthful as I tried to swallow. I eventually vomited the green beans back onto my plate. My mother came over, saw what I had done, and began to yell, "You ungrateful little shit, look at what you did! Look at it!"

I looked down at my plate of food, and she hammer-fisted me on the back of my head, slamming my face onto the table. My nose began to bleed. So now I had blood and green bean vomit on my food. She scolded me, "Get the fuck in the bathroom and clean your face!" I went to the bathroom, washed my face and hands, and shoved some toilet paper up my nostrils to stop my nose from bleeding. My mother yelled again, "Hurry the fuck up and get your ass back in here and eat so you can take your ass to bed!"

I returned to the table and just stood there looking at my plate. My mother did not fix me a new plate of food again. She shouted, "Sit your ass down and eat!" I began to cry as I pointed at my plate; my dinner was ruined. She grabbed me by the hair, pulled me over to the table, and shoved me down into my chair. "I don't have fucking food to waste," she yelled, "You better eat that shit!" My little brother began to cry as he watched me eat my vomit and blood-ruined dinner. After a few minutes, my mother came over and removed him from the table, allowing him to eat his dinner on the living room floor.

My mother then turned and walked down the hallway to her bedroom. I peeked down the hallway to make sure she was not standing there. I got up from the table and rushed my plate into the kitchen. I opened the cabinet below the sink where we kept the trash can and scraped what little food I had left into the trash. I put my plate back on the table and sat down. My mother returned a few minutes later, took my plate off the table, and yelled, "Take your ass to bed!" I went to my room and cried myself to sleep. I was awakened hours later as my mother came into my room, yelling and screaming, "You little mother-fucker!" She grabbed me by the hair and yanked me out of bed and onto the floor. I was terrified, in a daze, trying to wake up. She kicked me several times and yelled, "Get your ass up and go to the kitchen!"

I stumbled down the hall and into the kitchen. She grabbed me by my hair and pulled me over to the sink, throwing me onto the floor. The cabinets under the sink were opened; my mother found my food in the trash. She pointed and yelled, "Didn't I tell you I don't have any fucking food to waste? And you are going to throw that shit away and try to hide it? Come here!"

My mother grabbed me by the hair, dragged me over to the stove, and turned on the big electric eye. She pulled me up and placed my left hand over the eye. I remember grabbing the oven door handle with my other hand trying to pull myself away begging and screaming, "No! No! Please mom I'm sorry, I'm sorry," I could feel the eye on the stove go from warm to hot as I looked away. The heat, and the pain were excruciating. Then there was a knock at the front door. She threw me to the floor and yelled, "Get the fuck out of here and go to bed!" I ran to my room and once again cried myself to sleep.

As the years began to pass, I began to exhibit a lot of learning and behavioral problems at school. I began to have extreme outbursts of anger. I was not paying attention in class. I was talking back to teachers, fighting, and bullying other kids. I stabbed a kid with a pencil in class at Sunday school, and I slammed another kid's face into the water fountain, busting his mouth, and nose and knocking out his teeth. I had failing grades and was ditching school. I began hanging out with the wrong group of kids, stealing purses, and wallets, and breaking into cars. I was constantly being suspended from school.

Every time I was suspended, had detention, or a teacher, principal, or counselor called my parents, I would get my ass beat by both my mother and Rock. They would take turns coming into and out of my room like they were tag team wrestling. You are probably asking yourself, was it a beating? Or was it just a spanking? I GOT A BEAT DOWN. I WAS PUNCHED, KICKED, HAMMER FISTED, FRONT-HAND, and BACK-HAND SLAPPED. MY HAIR WAS PULLED. I WAS CHOKED, SPIT ON, AND SAT ON WITH MY ARMS TRAPPED AT MY SIDES AND PUNCHED IN THE FACE, and this was all from my mother. At times my mother would work herself up into this rage of fury before she beat me by yelling and screaming at me while pulling her hair, sometimes to the point of pulling out strands of her hair while punching and slapping herself in the face. Rock would always cuss me out and beat me with this thick-ass leather belt. In retrospect, my mother was broken and fucked up. I felt like behind most of those beatings were the frustration, shame, and embarrassment of having a black child and my father leaving her while she was pregnant with me. As for Rock, I felt like behind most of his beatings were also the embarrassment of having to raise another man's black child, the war he served in, and whoever else fucked him up when he was younger.

As a result of all of this, I grew up hating myself. I hated my skin color. I hated my hair. I hated being black. I had other mixed African-American and Mexican-American cousins, but they were all "High yellow." My mother loved them, often referring to them as Mijo and Mija (Son & daughter) while hugging them and kissing them. My mother often bragged about how cute they were when they were little and then how beautiful they became as they got older. My cousins and I got along great. I was close to my cousins, Marcel and Royce, and close to my cousins Rosemarie and Joe. However, deep down inside, I was very envious of them, all of them. I was jealous of their light skin and their light eyes. I was envious that both of their African-American Fathers were in their lives. Still, most of all, I was jealous of the love and admiration my mother had for them.

I'M GOING TO KILL MY PARENTS

Years later and many, many beatings later, I became a teenager. About 15 years old. I was washing and drying clothes—one of my many chores. I was treated like a slave in their home. I washed clothes and hung them up on the clothesline, and dried clothes in the dryer. I folded and put away my clothes along with my younger brother's and sister's clothes. I mowed and edged the front and backyard lawn. I pulled weeds from the flower beds. I fed the dogs. I picked up the dog droppings. I also threw out the trash and cut and stacked firewood. When our mother was out with her girlfriend, I would have to make dinner for my little brother, little sister, myself, and sometimes Rock. After we ate, I would wash the dishes, make sure my little brother and sister had their baths, and help them get their school clothes ready for the next day.

On this particular day, I finished a load of laundry. I put the clothes that needed drying in the dryer and hung the rest of the clothes on the clothesline. My mother came outside and began to look for something on the clothesline. She did not find what she was looking for, so she went into the garage and opened the dryer as I was putting another load of clothes into the washing machine. My mother was rummaging through the clothes for a minute when she pulled her bra out of the dryer. She walked over to me and yelled, "You dried my good bra!" And she slapped me across the face with it.

Let me paint a brief picture. Around this time, I was about 5ft 9in tall—a size 12 shoe and about 180lbs. My mother was about 5ft 1in and fat. So, when she slapped me across the face with her bra, something in me snapped. I dropped the clothes I was putting into the washing machine as I turned and faced her. My fists were balled up. I took a couple of steps forward and got really close to her, staring down at her face. She just looked at me and shouted, "What are you going to do, are you going to hit me? Do you think you're tough? Do you think you're grown now? Do you think you're a man? You aren't shit! You don't even have hair on your dick yet! As a matter of fact, you're going to grow up to be nothing but a sorry ass nigger just like your father!" She turned and walked away. I just stood there. I was furious! I could feel tears rolling down my face. It was the first time I felt like I actually wanted to kill my mother.

I began to walk out of the garage heading to my bedroom when my mother came back outside. She hugged me and told me she was sorry for what she said. I did not hug her back. I was still fucked up from being called a "Sorry ass nigger" by my mother. She got angry at my rejection and began to cuss me out some more. I don't even remember hearing what she said. I was in a trance or a zone of some sort. I could see her lips moving but I could hear nothing.

I turned and walked back into the garage. We had an old butcher knife we kept in one of the cabinets. We used it to cut miscellaneous things outside. I took the knife and put it in the waistband of my soccer shorts and covered it with my T-shirt. About this time, Rock came walking out into the backyard and asked my mom what she was yelling about. My mother lied and told him that I tried to hit her. Rock shouted, "Boy, bring your ass out here!" I came out and stood in the opening of the first garage bay door.

As I stood there, I could remember that it was hot outside. It was summer vacation, yet I don't remember feeling the sun on my skin. I don't remember hearing anything. I just remember standing there staring at Rock. My gaze was laser-focused on him. Like a movie in slow motion, my mind replayed this picture frame by frame of how I was going to stab Rock. Rock did not say anything. He just stared back. I stood there waiting for him to walk up to me and reach for me, to lunge at me, to grab at me as he had done many times before. My mind kept replaying an image of me shoving the knife into and through his Adams Apple. But he did not do anything. He just stood there. It seemed like the stare-down lasted forever. After about a minute, he shouted, "When you're done hanging up these clothes, go to your fucking room, your grounded!" I did not even touch the rest of the clothes. I did not go back into the garage. I went to my room, sat and waited.

I waited for him to come into my room with that thick-ass leather belt. I took the knife from my waistband and leaned it against the wall, blade down, handle up, next to my bed where I was sitting. I sat at the edge of my bed, waiting for hours. It was bright and sunny when I went to my room. It was now pitch-black outside. Rock worked the graveyard shift from 10 pm to about 10 am. So, it must have been around 9 pm. I remember hearing the shower running as he got ready for work. A few minutes later, my bedroom door opened. I grabbed the knife.

Rock was wearing his work uniform, blue mechanic coveralls. He leaned his upper body in through the doorway, leaning in far enough past my desk to peek at me sitting on the bed. I could feel my skin get hot. I could feel the adrenaline rush; he quickly said, "Go to bed" and flicked off the light switch as he closed my bedroom door. I did not sleep. I could not sleep. I was shaking from the surge of adrenaline. I remember sitting there all night, holding the knife.

As the years went on, my mother and Rock would still cuss at me and hurl abusive, profane, and prejudiced insults. My mother tried to instigate many fights between Rock and me, but Rock did not fall for it. He just left me alone. We would talk much shit back and forth to each other, which always keep me grounded but as long as he did not put his hands on me, I was okay with that. I often wondered if Rock saw the imprint of the knife. I wonder if my mother saw the imprint of the knife too. I wonder... who left my mother a broken woman.

LIFE GOES ON

I never got my ass beat for that day, and I never got my ass beat again after that day. Rock never touched me again. My mother never slapped me again. I still acted out; I had a lot of behavioral, emotional, and anger issues. Instead, I was grounded. A LOT! I was kept away from family members, mainly my grandmother. I would be grounded for 5, 6, and 7 months at a time: no birthday celebrations, no Christmas celebrations. I remember one Thanksgiving at my grandmother's house; the whole family was there. The family ate together at one table, while I was seated by myself at a different table facing the corner. At home, I was made to stand in the corner for hours at a time with no dinner for days. My little brother and I used to sneak food and feed each other dinner from our mouths whenever this punishment took place.

A day in the corner started as soon as we got home from school. We came in the door at about 2:30 pm and stood in the corner until bedtime at 9 pm. No dinner. No water. We were lucky to use the bathroom. A punishment of this type was for as long as Rock felt; typically, every day for a couple of months. If I were in the corner, my little brother would take food from his dinner plate, shove as much as he could fit into his mouth, quickly walk over to me and spit the food into the palm of my hand. I would promptly shove the food into my mouth and eat. When my little brother was in the corner with the same type of punishment, I would do the same for him. This went on for years.

On months when you did not have to stand in the corner, you had to sit in your room and write sentences. The sentences would be about whatever Rock dictated- "I will pay attention to my parents and not misbehave," or "I will Pay attention in school and get better grades," or something along those lines. And the number of sentences you had to write was the actual punishment. At times it would be three thousand sentences, five thousand sentences, or ten thousand sentences for me, and a couple of hundred times for my little brother. This went on for years.

I had a few good times in between the abuse. I got my driver's license and was fixing up a 1970 Chevelle. I was trying to date girls, and I tried out for football. I played summer league basketball, ran track, and worked at Long John Silver's during my senior year. I also participated in and won my senior talent show. I was trying to be an average teenager, but there was no longer anything average about me. I was badly damaged, but I did not realize exactly how damaged I was.

MY
BIOLOGICAL FATHER

My biological father. His name was Joe. He was African-American. He left me broken without even knowing he broke me. He never came around. I never got to meet him. I never knew anything about him. The most my mother told me about my father was that he was a pimp, and after she gave birth to me at the hospital, he brought two of his hoes up there to show me off. I never got to ask him any questions. I did not see a picture of my father until 2011. (I was born in 1974) I found the African-American side of my family, and my uncle showed me a picture of my dad. I never knew my dad, but I needed him. I required him desperately growing up. I needed to know what it meant to be black. I needed to know how to "Move" like a black man and how to think like a black man. I needed black culture and black awareness. I'm not saying that I would have gotten all of this from my father. After all, he never came to see me, but at least I would have gotten to see who I came from. I would have gotten to see a face that looked like mine, my resemblance. I desperately needed a face that looked like mine at home.

I hated my skin color, my hair, and everything about myself. The majority of Mexican-American kids at school and in my neighborhood wanted nothing to do with me because I was "Black," and the "Black" kids, the few that were there, wanted nothing to do with me because I was Mexican-American and considered "White-washed," because I did not talk like them. I had no black culture. No swag. It was times like this I wished my father would come and take me away. As a young Blackman, I was lost. Eventually, sometime during the 9th grade, I had become so depressed that I attempted suicide by sticking my head into our oven and inhaling the gas fumes, but I only passed out. I was awakened by my mother, kicking me and yelling," Get your fucking ass up off the floor!"

So, it was now my senior year at Roosevelt High School. I was sixteen years old. Lunchbreak was about to end, so I began heading toward my next class. A classmate of mine came up to me and said, "Hey James, your dad is looking for you." I said, "What?" I thought to myself, what the hell was Rock doing up here? He has never come to my school before. I asked, puzzled, "My dad?" He said, "Yeah, your dad Joe." I froze. I believed him because I never spoke of my dad's name to anyone. I felt my heart drop.

I began to turn my head quickly and scan around the campus. He said, "Yeah, your dad was across the street at Whimpy's (A hole in wall burger place), asking if anyone knew his son, James Bass. I ran back across the street to look for you on Senior Patio, but you were not there." I told him, "Thanks." I ran across the street and down the corner to Whimpy's. I looked and looked, but I did not see any adult black man. He was gone. Just that quick, he left. As I walked home from school. My mind was racing. I was angry, sad, and confused. When I got home, my mother was there, and I told her what had taken place. She tried to hide her initial reaction of shock and anger, but it was too late. I could see this news disturbed her. She said, "Go and tell Rock." I asked, "What for? This doesn't have anything to do with him." She yelled, "Rock is your father. He has been providing and taking care of you since you were 5 yrs. old." I rolled my eyes, scoffed, and said, "Whatever." I walked into the living room. Rock was sitting in his recliner, drinking a beer, and watching his favorite T.V show Archie Bunker. I said, "Hey Kane (A nickname my brother and I began to call him years earlier so we would not have to call him dad) my dad came up to the school looking for me today." Rock replied, "And?" I said, "I'm just telling you because mom told me to." I turned around and went to my room and shut the door.

The next morning was Saturday. We woke up to the front window of our house being smashed. Someone had thrown a brick through the window. I walked over as Rock picked up the brick and showed it to my mother. I could see that there was writing on the brick in bold black ink, but I could not make out what it said. Before I could read it, Rock put the brick at his side and said, "What are you being so fucking nosey for?" My mother told me to mind my own fucking business. I just scoffed and went back to my room.

We moved into that house when I started the 7th grade. I was now going to graduate from high school in a couple of months. Nothing like that ever happened before. Our home was burglarized once shortly after moving in, but that was years earlier. I think it was my father, Joe. I can't prove it. But that is what I think. I think he was sending a message to my mother. I wonder... who left my father a broken man

THE SETUP FOR MEETING WIFEY

It was now June of 1992. I made it! I don't know how, but I graduated from Roosevelt high school! My next plan was to move out of that shit-hole excuse of a home. The goal was to move in with my Abuelita (Grandmother). It was going to be hard; I could not just pick up and leave. I was 17 years old. I was still a minor. I was not going to turn 18 until November. Five more months of this shit! I told myself, "You have been dealing with this since you were 4 years old. You can hang in there for five more months! But how? What the hell was I going to do all day?" At least I had school five days a week to escape home life, and now that was gone. I had a three-year routine while at Roosevelt. I would get up at 6 am, get dressed, leave at 7 am, and walk ½ mile to school and buy breakfast. I would joke around with my friends, harass my teachers, mess around and make out with girls, and ditch classes I did not like. Without even realizing it, Roosevelt High had become my haven. It was my sanctuary five days a week, and even during the summer. (I've had summer school every summer since the 9th grade). So, I decided I would get a job.

I called my Tia (Aunt). She worked for the City of Fresno in the Parks and Recreation department. She got me a job for the summer as an Assistant Lifeguard at a local city playground called Frank H Ball. Great! My plan was coming together. I had my driver's license, I had a car, and the playground was on the West Side of Fresno, and since Rock and my mother hated "niggers", they would not be anywhere around. I was good!

My new job was cool. It was like high school. I was working with these cool ass dudes—one black dude, we called him J. The other was a white boy, we called him Brian. J was a crazy-ass brother that talked about women, cars, money, and sports all day long. Brian was the same, except that he had a brand-new Kawasaki Ninja motorcycle, so he talked about bikes as well. The transition from high school to Frank H was seamless. The job was from July through September. I worked in a little cage-like office next to the pool. I made sure the kids, teens, and adults paid to get in, and when one of the lifeguards on duty needed to take their lunch break, I would rotate out and take over guard duty watching the people as they swam. The way I saw it was, I'm seventeen and getting paid to watch and flirt with some of the most beautiful black girls and women at the pool all day long. J and Brian agreed.

After a couple of weeks on the job, I noticed a little boy, around 7 years old. (I will call him Loner.) He would come in with a large group of boys. They would all come in, pay 25 cents, jump into the pool, and have a blast. But Loner never paid. He never swam. He would hang around in front of the office by himself and wait for his friends to finish swimming. I noticed this for a couple of weeks—several times during the week. The next day they arrived at the pool and he hung around outside, as usual, so I asked him, "Hey man, how come you don't go in and swim with your friends?" He did not answer me. I asked him, "Do you know how to swim?" He said, "Yeah, I know how." I asked again, "So how come you don't swim with your friends?" He said, "Because my mom forgot to give me some money." I asked, "She forgot for two weeks in a row?"

Loner gave me a look as if to say, "Nigga Please!" I chuckled and said, "Oh, ok. I tell you what". I pulled a dollar out of my pocket. I said, "Here you go, buddy." I tried to hand it to him, but he did not take it. I said, "Ok, I get it. I'm a stranger. Well, check this out." He watched as I opened the cash register and put the dollar in. I said, "That's for you. Now you can swim all week." I saw him try to contain his smile behind his little tough guy face. I could tell he was trying to figure me out. He just stood there. (I just felt terrible for the kid). So, I had to ante up large fees. I said, "Matter of fact," I took the dollar out and showed him a $5.00 bill. I put the $5.00 in the register and said, "Now, you can swim all month!" Loner just stood there in shock.

I could see that he did not know how to take this act of kindness. He slowly turned around and began to leave the pool, walking out of the gate. I thought he was going home. I stood up and kind of shouted, "Hey, where are you going?" I did not get an answer. Instead, a few seconds later, Loner came running through the gate, exclaiming in a playful tone, "Aaaaaahhhhhhh," as he jumped, cannonball style, into the pool. All of his friends yelled, yeah! Yeah! As they began to give each other hi-fives and hugs. Loner came every day for a couple of weeks and swam with his friends. He didn't say much of anything to me. He would just run by the office and jump into the pool. He had a blast.

Three weeks went by, and Loner was hanging out in front of the office again. Only this time, right in front of the office. He didn't say anything, but he definitely wanted me to notice him. So I said, "Hey, what's up? How come you're not swimming?" He answered, "Because you're not supposed to swim if you are going to eat." I looked confused. I said, "No, I think it's, you're not supposed to swim right after you eat." He just looked at me, thinking about what I said. I asked him, "So what did you eat?" He sounded a little embarrassed, "Nothing yet." I put two and two together and quickly played it off. I could smell food in the air. I did not know what it was, but it was close, and it smelled good. So I asked Loner, "Hey man, you smell that? It smells good!" Loner quickly perked up with excitement. He said, "They are making Frito Boats across the playground at the gym." I said, "Frito Boats? What's a Frito Boat?" He looked at me as if I had just crawled out of a cave. He said, "Maaan, you ain't never had a Frito boat?!" I said no, "What is it?" Loner said, "Shit… They put a bunch of Frito chips in a bowl. Then they put a bunch of taco meat with beans over that. Then they put melted nacho cheese on top of that!" I said, "Oh yeah? How big are these boats?" He said, "They are big, and they give you a lot. I can barely eat one by myself." I said, "Ok, ok, how much are they?" He said, "$2.50," all excited. I reached in my pocket and gave him $5.00. I said, "Okay, get one for you and me." He said, "Okay," with a big smile on his face. He snatched the money out of my hand and took off, running. I watched as he ran around the gate and to the gym: no socks, no shoes, and no shirt, just his black swim shorts.

I was filling out some paperwork when he returned about 2 minutes later, carrying these two big Frito boats with nacho cheese sauce all around his mouth. I said, "Damn, you weren't kidding! These things look good." He said, "Yeah, taste good too!" I thanked him. He looked at me, puzzled. He asked, "Why are you thanking me? You paid for them." I said, "Yeah, but you went to go and get them." He thought about it for a second as he shoveled a bunch of beans, meat, and melted cheese into his mouth with some chips and said," Oh yeah," in agreement. We sat there for a few minutes, not saying anything, just stuffing our faces with this delicious food when Loner asked me, "Are you thirsty?" I said, "Yeah, how about you? He nodded and said, "They got sodas over there." I asked what kind. He ran down the list of sodas with enthusiasm. "They got 7up, Orange, Grape, Pepsi, Dr. Pepper…" I said, "I will take an Orange soda." He said, "I will take a 7up." I laughed. I asked, "Okay. How much are the sodas?" He said, "25 cents." I said, "25 cents!?" Loner must have thought my tone implied that I would say no because he put his head down and replied, "Yeah, I guess it is a lot for a can of soda." I said, "Shit! That's a deal. They are 75 cents at the vending machines." He perked up with a big smile. I gave him $1.00 and said, "Get me two orange sodas please." He looked at me, paused for a second, and asked, "Can I get two too?" I said, "You can if you want." He got a big smile on his face and took off faster than he had before.

Loner came walking back with a big smile on his face carrying four cans of soda with cheese sauce still covering his mouth. It was hilarious. We sat there and ate as a line of kids began to form outside as they waited for the pool to open. Loner's friends saw him eating. One of his friends looked at him and said, "Hey, man! Where did you get all of that?" Loner pointed at me as he drank down his soda. His friends said, "Aw, man, you lucky."

I watched in amazement as Loner shot gunned his 7up. I mean, he drank the whole can in one shot, and when he was done, he let out a colossal burp. I said, "Damn man, I think you just lost 4 pounds." He laughed. I asked him, "How can you drink a soda like that?" He said, "7up is my favorite." I said, "Yeah, but doesn't that burn your throat?" He chuckled and said, "It's not hot!" I said, "Yeah, I know it's not hot, but the carbonation, doesn't that burn?" He looked puzzled as he repeated the word, "Carbonation? What's that?" I said, "It's what gives soda its bubbles." He said, "Oh,"…then he asked, "You can't drink a whole soda like that?" I said, "Nope." He asked, "Why not? I said, "Because it burns my throat." He laughed and said, "But you're big, and I'm small." I asked, "So, because I'm big, it should not burn?" He said, "Yeah," laughing. I said, "Okay, let me try."

I opened my orange soda and took about three good chugs before my eyes began to water. My face was getting red as I took the 4th swallow. I quickly put the can down on the table. My face looked as if it were going to pop. My eyes were extremely watery. Loner began to laugh hard. He was in tears. I began to laugh as I told him, "Damn, man. That shit burns!" I wiped the tears from my eyes. Loner died with laughter as he pointed at me. I began to laugh as well. I pictured how silly I must have looked to a little kid.

After Loner was done laughing. He began to eat some more of his Frito boat, and he asked me, "You're not from around here, huh?" I said, "Yeah. I live here in Fresno." He said, "No, I mean, you're not from the West Side." I said, "No, I'm not." He said, "I know because you're nice, and you talk funny." I chuckled and asked, "I talk funny? He laughed as he shoved some chips into his mouth and said, "Yeah, like a goofy white boy." "Hahaha," I laughed, "A goofy white boy?" He laughed harder and said, "Yeah!" I asked him playfully, "Hey man, are you laughing at me or with me?" He said, "Both!" And we both cracked up laughing.

I said, "Boy, you are cold! But at least I don't have cheese-boogers running down my nose." He looked up paranoid and said, "What!" I pointed to a mirror behind the office door. He got up and looked in the mirror and shouted, "Maaan! How long have those been there?" I said, "For a while," as I handed him a napkin laughing. He laughed and asked, "Why didn't you tell me?" I said, "I thought you were saving those cheesy boogers for later." He repeated, "Saving them for later?" I said, "Yeah, to eat with the rest of your Frito's." We were cracking up. He said, "Naw, man, there're girls around here." I asked, "Girls? What do you know about girls?" He said, "Man, I got all the girls." I just chuckled and shook my head.

We laughed, joked, and clowned on each other, and his friends for the rest of that afternoon. We had a blast. This process repeated itself for the rest of June into the middle of July. Then it stopped. Just as quickly as he showed up, Loner disappeared. I waited for him to come in day after day, week after week, but he never showed up. I began to worry. I began to wonder what happened to Loner.

MEETING MY WIFE PT.1

The beginning of August came around, and I still had not seen Loner. Around the 2nd week of August, this beautiful Black woman came walking into the pool area. I could not take my eyes off her. I had never seen such a gorgeous black woman in person before. Up to that point, all of the beautiful black women that I had seen were on the T.V shows Soul Train and Yo! M T.V raps. She walked over to J and Brian and asked them something. J pointed over to me at the office and this gorgeous black woman began walking toward me. I got nervous; I could feel my skin flush. Her beauty was intimidating.

Her skin was a sun-kissed caramel color. She had full, soft-looking lips—a cute little button nose along with almond shaped-Chinese-like eyes. My eyes quickly focused on her boobs. They were so lovely. Then my eyes made their way down to her small waistline and that fat booty of hers. I caught my wondering eyes and quickly focused my gaze back onto her face, hoping she did not see me undress her with my eyes. She just smiled as she walked up to me. She smelled amazing. I will never forget the scent of Cesar's Woman perfume that radiated off of that gorgeous frame of hers. Then she spoke....and I came back down to earth.

She asked, "Are you, James?" "Yes," I nervously answered. She asked, "Have you seen my nephew?" I looked puzzled. "Your nephew? Who is your nephew?" She said his name. I still looked confused. She said, "I just wanted to come by and see if he was here. He talks about you all of the time. He says you are a nice guy. I wanted to say thank you for looking out for him."

As she was speaking, I realized she was talking about Loner. I said, "Oh yeah. No problem. He's a good kid."

She said, "I'm Crystal. I'm his aunt," and she extended her hand. I shook her hand and said, "It's nice to meet you." I told her I had not seen Loner for a couple of weeks. I was worried and wondering about him. She just stared at me as I spoke. I could tell she was studying me. She said, "I have not seen him today. I've been to my sister's house, but she is not there. I will try her later on."

Crystal thanked me once again, then she turned and began to walk away. I said, "When you see him tell him I said hi." She just turned, paused for a second at the gate, smiled a warm smile, and left.

THE POOL PARTY,
MEETING MY WIFE PT.2

Towards the end of August, the playground was having an end-of-the-summer pool party. The pool was closing in early September because school would be starting. The playground, basketball gym, picnic area, and pool were packed. There was music, food, and black people everywhere. It was the first time in my life I experienced black culture in person. It was great! Beautiful black women everywhere! I was sitting in the lifeguard chair/tower watching over the kids swimming when I heard someone shout my name, "James!" I looked around. "James, James!" they called. I looked towards the entrance of the pool, and it was Loner. He was waving. And he had a massive smile on his face. I smiled as I waved back. Loner pointed down the entrance as if to say, look! Look! Then Crystal came walking in. She was wearing a real tight-fitting swimsuit. My tongue almost fell out of my mouth as my jaw dropped. Loner saw me and laughed. I climbed down from the chair and told Brian I was taking my break. Brian got up into the seat to take over. I walked over to Loner and Crystal and said Hi. Crystal smiled and said, "Hi." She was holding one of her daughter's hands. It was her oldest. She was eight. And she was carrying another little girl in her arms. It was her youngest daughter, she was five, and she was asleep. I asked Crystal if she wanted to sit down in the office. She said, "No, thank you, I'm going to sit with my feet in the pool and watch Loner and my daughter swim. I said, "Okay."

I watched Crystal walk to the edge of the pool, and it was as if everything slowed down. I never, in my life, up to that point, had seen an ass as spectacular as hers. Her booty seemed to defy the laws of physics as she walked. It didn't even jiggle when she walked, it "Quivered like it had the chills" simply amazing! I took in the full sight of Crystal and all of her splendor, not knowing if I would ever see her again. She was in great shape. She was about 135 lbs. and tall for a woman, around 5ft 6in. Her legs were very thick and well defined, and her make-up and hair were flawless. I was in la-la land staring at her when Loner came running up and said, "Hi!" He gave me a big hug. I kneeled and asked, "Hey, buddy, where have you been?" Loner told me he had been at his grandmother's house for a while. She lived far from the playground, and she would not take him to the pool. He was explaining everything he had been doing while at his grandmother's house. Then he said, "Guess what? My Aunt wants your phone number!"

I froze. I said, "What?" Loner nodded with excitement and repeated, "My aunt wants your phone number." I asked, "Your aunt?" He nodded. I pointed and said, "Crystal?" He laughed and said, "Yeah!" I said, "Shit! Let me write that down right now!" He laughed. I wrote my phone number down on a piece of paper and gave it to him. He took off running. Crystal must have left for the gym with her girls because when I watched Loner run away, he ran to the gym. Loner came running back after a few minutes and said, "She will call you later." "Cool," I replied. Later on, Crystal returned with a basketball she had won at a contest for the kids at the gym. She walked up to me and asked if I could hold it for her until she left. I took the ball from her, trying to touch her hands in the process. She turned and walked away. I waited for Crystal to come back that afternoon. She never came. I thought, oh well, she has my number and I looked forward to her call.

It was now September. The pool had closed, and school had started. I had not heard from Crystal. No phone call, nothing. I had started a job with the school district as a Substitute Teacher's Aide. So, I was still working, making money, and staying out of the house as long as possible. In late September, I was at one of our local malls. I was going to Footlocker to buy myself a pair of Jordan's. I was walking down the busy mall when I noticed this woman in the distance. I looked harder, peering through the people as they passed. It was Crystal! She was in one of the stores. I walked up to her and said, "Hi." She looked up, smiled, and said, 'Hi." Her smile was like sunshine. I asked, "Do you remember me?" She said, "Yes, you're James from the pool." I laughed and said, "Oh, okay, you do remember." She chuckled as she shook her head.

There was an awkward silence for a moment as I watched her look through some clothes. So, I politely said, "You have a funny way of asking for a number and then not using it." She looked up, puzzled, and said, "Excuse me?" I got nervous as I said, "My number...You asked for it...But you have not called me." She stopped what she was doing. She took a couple of steps toward me. She was now right in front of me, about ten inches from my face. She asked me softly, "Who said I wanted your number?" "You did," I replied. She just looked at me, so I continued, "At the pool party." I took one step back to create some distance between us. She took that space away as she got closer to me again and asked delicately, "I did? When?" I could feel her boobs against my chest; I was so nervous but excited at the same time.

I said, "Well, you didn't. Loner came up to me and told me you wanted my number. So I gave it to him, to give it to you." She took a step back, looked away, and giggled to herself as she shook her head. I said, "You didn't, did you?" She said, "No, I never did. Loner came up to me and told me the same thing. He ran up to me when I was at the gym and said that you wanted my phone number. I just told him, "boy, get out of here." She and I laughed as we realized that Loner was playing matchmaker. So I asked, "Well, can I have your number?" Crystal paused for a second and said, "No, but I will take yours." I took out a pen and wrote my number down on a piece of paper. I gave it to her and asked, "You're going to call me this time, right?" She said, "Maybe," and smiled. I told her okay and said how nice it was to see her again as I turned and walked away. A few weeks later, Crystal called.

A PEOPLE BREAKER

I often reminisce about the beautiful memory of how I met my wife, reliving that summer over and over in my mind. At that pool, I now realize, when Crystal came walking in, that was God delivering my angel to me. Whatever God you believe in, whatever higher power or universal being you pray to; that was them providing my angel. My very own angel.

I would never have thought in a million years, nor could I have foreseen how despicable I would treat my angel in the years to come. I went from the abused to the abuser. I would cheat with other women and not come home for days, weeks, or months. I would yell at her, cuss at her and call her a bitch. I would push her, choke her, and punch and kick holes in the doors and walls.

I remember one horrendous outburst. It was the summer of 1993; I was 18 years old. Crystal and I had gotten our first apartment together. It was a charming apartment. It had two bedrooms and two bathrooms. It was a single level with a fireplace and had an attached garage with a swimming pool. It should have been a happy occasion for us, but for me, it was not. I don't even recall how the argument started, but I am 100% certain it was my fault. I began to yell and cuss at Crystal. We were in the kitchen. She left the kitchen and headed toward the living room. I grabbed her by the back of her shirt and yanked her hard, backward towards the hallway. She flew back, falling, hitting the back of her head on the floor. She got up dazed, yelling for her girls to stay in their bedroom as she stumbled, trying to run down the hallway. She ran into our bedroom and tried to shut the door behind her, but I kicked the door inward, and she fell backward into the wall. She was crying, screaming, and begging me to calm down, but I could not. My rage was uncontrollable. It was like someone flipped a light switch. All I could feel was darkness and destruction, and unfortunately, Crystal was the unintended target.

She got up from the floor and jumped across our bed, running into the master bathroom. She tried again to shut the door attempting to lock me out; however, I kicked in that door as well and her attempt became abortive. When I kicked the door inward, the force from my kick knocked her backward into the wall, causing Crystal to hit the back of her head a second time. She fell to the floor. Crystal lay in a daze, covering her face with her hands while trying to catch her breath. The force from the impact knocked the wind out of her. I began to punch holes into the wall just above her head. I can vividly remember the top of her head and her hair covered in white powder from the sheet rock as I pulled my fist from the wall with each punch. Then I turned and began to kick the cabinet doors below the sink. Crystal managed to crawl into the shower and close the door in an attempt to seek some sort of refuge. After destroying the cabinet doors, I began to punch the mirror repeatedly above the sink while shouting, "I hate you! I fucking hate you!"

The glass was falling everywhere. I remember seeing flashes of my mother's face in the reflection of the mirror. Out of the corner of my eye, I noticed Crystal was no longer where I last saw her. I turned around, and I could see a distorted image of her through the frosted shower glass door. She was cowering on the floor. I punched through the door, causing the glass to fly everywhere. Crystal stood up. I will never forget the look of terror on her face as she stood there, struggling with the probability that her life was about to end. She extended her arms outward, shaking her head. I reached in and grabbed her by the throat with my right hand, trying to pull her out. As I began to squeeze, blood squirted onto the side of her face. I felt an immediate loss of energy. I lost my balance and fell backward against the counter.

There was blood everywhere, on the counter, the walls, and the floor; it looked like a murder scene. My right fist was blown open and mangled. Big shards of glass from the mirror and shower door were embedded in my fist, and I was bleeding profusely. Crystal got herself underneath my arm, held me up, and she raised my right arm above our heads in an attempt to slow the bleeding. I can remember blood from my fist running down my arm as we stumbled down the hallway, trying to make it into the garage. I lost consciousness. I remember waking up on the kitchen floor. Crystal had wrapped my hand in a towel and tied a makeshift tourniquet around my arm. She was desperately trying to drag me across the floor, from the kitchen to the garage door. She was crying, shouting, "Get up James, please get up. I can't lift you."

I managed to get on my hands and knees and crawl into the garage. She helped me up into her jeep and rushed me to the emergency room. As the nurses took me in, I passed out once again. I woke up to a doctor putting stitches between the knuckles of my middle and ring finger. The doctor asked Crystal what happened, she said, "I don't know. I came home and found him this way.

Like I said at the beginning of the book, **I was a pile of shit with shoes**. I hated the person that I had become, but it was like I could not stop. I began drinking heavily to chase my troubles away, but I only felt worse when the bottles were empty. Eventually, I had another suicide attempt at the age of 29. I swallowed a handful of Tylenol pills and washed them down with a bottle vodka. My wife found me when she returned home from her walk. I had blacked out and was covered in vomit on the bathroom floor. I did not understand where all the anger and rage were coming from, but I was full of it, and it was spewing out. My anger would continue from 1993- 2007. There were some times in between those years when it was peaceful. But the damage had already been done. I had broken my wife's spirit. I had hurt and changed the way her daughters viewed me. I had also changed the way they viewed their mother. I changed the trajectory of the lives of these three individuals. I had become a "people breaker" just like my mother and stepfathers. For this, to my wife and her daughters, I genuinely and whole-heartedly apologized.

I never saw the break in my wife. I don't think any husband ever does. Crystal still loved me. Throughout all her tears and pains, she never stopped loving me, as well as her daughters. Many years later, in 2004, she started a business. In 2005 we got married. I had begun to get my act together. My violent outbursts had calmed down towards Crystal, but I was still vengefully furious. I now began to fight with grown men on my job, and with grown men out in public, severely beating them up and sending many of them to the hospital emergency room. I stopped cheating but I was still flirting. I could not understand why. During an argument, I dared to ask my wife, "If I'm such a horrible person, why are you still with me? Why do you still love me?" Through her tears, she uttered a sentence that rattled my core. She said, "I love you not for the person you are, but for the man you will become."

I'm going to repeat that. Crystal told me, **I love you not for the person you are... but for the man you will become**. Something about those words pierced my soul. I was a bus driver at the time. I drove around for weeks with that phrase replaying in my mind. The painful look on her face when she said it was burned into my memory. Those words I will never forget. My mind flashed every bad thing that had been done to me during my childhood. Then it replayed everything that I had done to her and everything that I put her daughters through. I realized I had become no better than my mother, I had become no better than Sid, neither had I become better than Rock. So, in the summer of 2007, I stopped. It was a challenging transition to make, but I stopped all the abuse. I stopped all of my cheating and flirting. I stopped everything. I had a long talk with my wife. I apologized for everything that I put her through. I apologized for everything that I had done to her. I also attempted to apologize to her daughters, but they were not receptive to my words at that time; I didn't blame them. I promised my wife that no matter how long it took, I would make her whole again. I promised that I would never leave her side.

Little did I know that the damage had already been done. **I never sought counseling for my wife or myself.** Furthermore, in an attempt **to conceal my shame and embarrassment**, for years, **I allowed my family and friends to think my wife was the problem.**

MY BROKEN WIFE. DEPRESSION, THE FIRST RIPPLE

n 2009, my wife's mood began to change. This angel of a person had become extremely verbally abusive. This woman that loved me, began to hate the sight of me. She began to lash out at me with venom and tell me things I never thought I would hear her say. The slightest thing would piss her off. She would tell me that she wished she never fucking met me. She wished she would have fucking left me years ago. She wished that my mother would have gotten a fucking abortion, wishing that I had never been born. She told me that she should have fucked all my friends while I was cheating on her. I could not believe the things she was saying to me. She had never spoken to me like this before. However, I understood where it was all coming from; I put her through hell, and now it was my turn to reap what I sowed. I was cool with that. Let me repeat….**I was cool with that**. I made her a promise. I understood that I had made my bed, and now I had to lie in it. So, I would just allow her to vent. Whenever she was feeling some type of way about me, I would just let her get whatever she had to say off her chest! I would listen quietly to how she felt. I would accept all of the painful things she had to say, and when she was done, I would apologize. I would apologize for the way I made her feel. I would apologize for all of the horrible things I put her through. I would begin to say to her, "I'm sorry," and she would interrupt by saying, "Yeah, you are sorry all right, just a sorry ass piece of shit. Just a worthless, sorry as nigga."

It's a lot to take in from your wife. It was not easy to hear, but I would just deal with it. I understood that this was part of the "Healing process" for her. I was right…in a sense. But also, very wrong. I started to purchase relationship books to try and help her during this process. I bought Men are from Mars, Women are from Venus, Relationship Rescue, and Loving one Another. I showed her the books and suggested we read them. Crystal told me, "Oh, now your black ass wants to read? Where were these books when you were terrorizing me? Read them by your fucking self. Read them so you can learn how to be a real fucking man and then take what you've learned and go share it with your other bitch because I'm through with you!" Crystal turned and walked into the bedroom, slamming the door and locking me out.

She would not speak to me for days, and weeks at a time. I would sleep in the living room on the couch, get up the next day, and go to work. When I would come home and walk into a room or pass her in the kitchen or hallway, she would look at me and scoff, roll her eyes, and mumble, "Sorry ass nigga." Although she would mumble these words under her breath, she would say them just loud enough for me to hear. I wouldn't react. I wouldn't say anything or answer her. I would just hurry up and get the hell out of her way. I didn't want to "Trigger" anything else.

I soon understood that just the mere sight of me was triggering these angry outbursts, so I only came into the home when necessary. I stayed out in the garage, and I slept in our car (A BMW Z4 Roadster, and I'm almost 6 ft. tall). I only came in to take a shower when I got home from work. I would fix myself something to eat and take my food out to the garage. Most of the time I would just purchase some fast food to avoid even coming into our home. I had some empty one-gallon plastic jugs in the garage. They were leftover plastic bottles of car detailing products. I would pee in them if I needed to use the bathroom, and if I had to take a doo-doo, I would wait until I got to work the next day.

This routine went on for several months, and off and on for several years. While I was in the garage, I spent a lot of time on YouTube. I watched countless hours of videos on relationships, the human mind, depression, anxiety, narcissistic behavior, PTSD, co-dependency, how men process emotion, how women process emotion, child development, and childhood abuse.... you get the picture. I learned a great deal about myself, my wife, and people in general. I discovered that I carried my childhood into my marriage without realizing it. Even more significant, I understood why.

One day, my wife came out to the garage. It was the middle of the summer. It was over 110 degrees outside, which meant it was hotter in the garage. Crystal banged on the door. I grabbed the remote and opened the garage. She walked over to the driver's window and said, "Come inside; it's too hot for you to be in here." She turned and walked away. She still had that look of disgust on her face when she spoke to me...but she spoke to me—no cuss words, no yelling, and no screaming. Not only did she speak, but she invited me into our home. I was grateful for her act of kindness. So I walked in, and Crystal began to apologize to me. She told me that she was angry and hurt at everything that I put her through. She apologized for the way she spoke to me. She apologized for the way she treated me. I was shocked and surprised, but happy. I told her that I understood and that she owed me no apology because it was not her fault. I was responsible for her feelings of pain, anger, and distrust. I kneeled and apologized once again. We cried as we held each other; I thought it was finally over…I was dead wrong.

REAL TALK, MY EPIPHANY

I'm going to break away from the story for a brief minute to talk to you fellas. I know many of you men are probably reading this and thinking… Invited you in? You live there too. You go to work, you pay the bills, and you let your wife treat you like a second-class citizen? Why don't you grow a pair of nuts and leave?

Well, I understand, and part of me felt like leaving, however, **this is my wife. I married her, I broke her, and I made a promise that "I would fix what I broke**." Please don't misunderstand what I am saying; there were plenty of occasions when I felt like leaving, like throwing in the towel. Me sitting in the garage was the least I could do compared to all that I put her through. Sitting in the garage alone for hours, days, weeks, and months at a time, helped me realize what my problem was as a young adult: I had no self-love, no self-worth, and very, very low self-esteem.

As a result of hating my skin color when I was younger, I grew up feeling like I was ugly and unattractive. I was very self-conscious about my appearance and thus became overly insecure. As I stated earlier, I hated being black. My subconscious feelings merged the abuse from Sid, Rock, and my mother with my skin color. I had concluded, subconsciously, that black equals ugly and I did not deserve respect or love. Therefore, no woman could or would ever love me for simply being me. So my constant cheating was me seeking approval and needing reassurance that I was not ugly. The many women I cheated with never quenched my frenzy or my need for comfort and acceptance, and after a while, I became addicted to the attention. I became addicted to feeling "loved and wanted."

I had a love for Crystal, who was my girlfriend at the time, but unfortunately, it was not enough. My addiction was too strong and had become uncontrollable. It felt good to be wanted. It felt good to be looked at with admiration. It felt good to be "Loved." Over these years, I got an overabundance of "love" from many different women. The "love" and attention slowly turned into arrogance, and I became remarkably conceited. As I stated earlier, I battled with this problem for 14 years, not realizing that all along, I was seeking the love that I never got from my mother.

You might be thinking, "Okay, that explains the cheating, but what about the physical abuse?"

It is no secret that the developmental stage of a child is crucial to whom they will become. Experts feel this stage is from birth through age five. Some argue it is from ages 0-3, but many agree that by age five, whatever environment the child has been brought up in will likely dictate what behavior or traits will be considered normal as the child grows up. For me, I normalized hate, violence, rage, and destruction. Destroying a person's self-worth, my woman's self-worth, was familiar because my self-worth had been destroyed by my mother. I had been unconsciously/subconsciously transferring the rage and vehemence I felt for my mother onto Crystal. Perhaps worst of all, buried deep into my psyche, was the subconscious belief of how black women were nothing but "worthless bitches and hoes." A belief that was drilled into me at an early age by my mother.

I no longer judge abusive men or men who cheat because **it is not who they are; it is their behavior that is wrong**. I don't condone their actions neither do I excuse mine; however, there are reasons for everything. I empathize with these men and their struggle because behind the destructive behavior is a simple need. These men, like myself, did not receive something at a crucial time, and they are desperately seeking it, without consciously knowing what they are searching for while destroying other people and loved ones in the process.

MEN, PLEASE SEEK PROFESSIONAL HELP! TALK TO A THERAPIST, A PSYCHOLOGIST, or a PSYCHIATRIST. THE EARLIER THE BETTER. *THERE IS NO SHAME IN THIS GAME.* YOU ARE NOT WEAK OR LESS OF A MAN FOR SEEKING HELP. THERE IS NO SUCH THING AS A CRAZY PERSON, ONLY CRAZY CIRCUMSTANCES THAT DRIVE PEOPLE INSANE.

DEPRESSION, FIRST WAVE

The years went on and Crystal and I had many good times, but she still struggled with our past. There were times she would become overly suspicious, feeling like I was seeing other women. She would lash out at me for no apparent reason. She started to throw things at me and would leave the apartment for hours at a time. Over the years, I became extremely frustrated at the way I was being treated. I began to lash out in defense shouting, "I already fucking apologized for that shit!"

I began to remind Crystal of the ways that I had changed but it was of no use. Crystal was on the attack. I suggested that we go for marriage counseling, and she said, "Why? I already feel like a fucking fool and a loser for staying with you. Now you want me to look like a fucking fool in front of someone else?" A couple of months later, I lost all composure. Everything I learned about her and myself went out the window. I was tired of being attacked. Five years had flown by, but to her, it was as if it were yesterday. I punched a hole in the bedroom door out of pure frustration, which sent Crystal into an even further tailspin. That one action re-confirmed to her that I had not changed and that I was the "Same old James." Her anger towards me started up all over again; however, this time, she asked for a divorce. Out of pure frustration, I agreed. I found an attorney. I got the paperwork, but I never filed, I never left. I was determined to keep my promise to her.

Eventually, my wife's depression became worse. I forgot to mention, that back in 2010, we worked at a job together. The job and company were horrible. For me, it was okay. I was used to the chaos. But for my wife, it was terrible. There was a female employee that was married to the father of Crystal's nephew (Loner's dad) and that female employee's sister worked there as well. The sister spread horrible family gossip throughout the warehouse regarding Crystal's childhood. It made my wife's anger, anxiety, and depression worse. So Crystal took her anger and frustration for that situation out on me as well. Eventually, Crystal had to be hospitalized for her depression. She got to a point at which she no longer wanted to live.

A couple of years had gone by and Crystal was in and out of the hospital, battling depression and suicidal thoughts. Each time she was admitted into the hospital, they kept her for no less than eight days. During that time, she was on a lot of different medications. I never left. I stayed with her. I was at the hospital every day during visiting hours. I was talking to her on the phone while I was at work. I worried about how she was doing. I worried about how she was being treated. Every time Crystal was discharged from the hospital, I made it a point to do something she loved. Such simple things included going to the park and feeding the ducks, going for walks and going to the movies. My wife had become self-conscious of her weight. She had gotten up to 196 pounds, a side effect of the anti-depressant medications she was taking. She became very self-conscious, believing that I would no longer find her sexy or attractive and that I would leave her. I never felt that way. I was never ashamed of her weight gain. I was just happy to have my wife home. I was delighted to have her back in my arms and the medication was helping. She was beginning to mellow out.

Eventually, Crystal became frustrated with her weight and became frustrated with the medications. She became determined to battle her depression another way. She became interested in homeopathic and Ayurveda remedies and became heavily involved in studying different plants, herbs, minerals, and supplements. I supported her on her new journey. Eventually, she became so good at it to the extent that against the doctor's orders, in October of 2014, she quit taking all of her medications. She went through a rough withdrawal period and began to lash out again. I just took it on the chin. Eventually, once the supplements and herbs began to get into her system regularly, she was okay. I mean, she was great. I began to take an interest in what she was doing. At first, I thought it was all a bunch of hype, but once she started to mellow out, I became impressed with everything she learned. We eventually got a gym membership. We were up at 3:30 am and at the gym at 4 am. She swam laps in the pool as I lifted weights. She felt great. We were doing great. Over the next year, she went from 196 lbs. down to 145 lbs. I was back in good shape, a solid 205 lbs. And we were getting along better than we ever had, but least did I know that the worst was yet to come.

My wife's depression never left, her mood had stabilized, but **WE NEVER SOUGHT THERAPY.** I thought she was better. She thought she was better. I was not going to "Rock the boat." We began to read all of the relationship books I had purchased, and we bought new relationship books to read as well. But the depression was still there. **SHE NEVER RECEIVED THERAPY.** Crystal's depression began to manifest itself in other ways. It went from angry outbursts to a shopping addiction.

DEPRESSION, SECOND WAVE

From 2015 to 2016, Crystal shopped. She shopped online and in person. She bought any and everything that she could. She bought tons of shoes, purses, bags, blouses, hats, scarves, gloves, boots, heels, jackets, bras, panties, dishes, pots, pans, furniture, DVDs, Blu-ray movies, a VCR, VHS tapes, (Yes, VCR's and VHS movies, a dead technology) weightlifting equipment… you get the picture. She reminded me of that song by the R&B singer, Blu Cantrell, "Hit Em Up Style." Her spending was out of control. She began to destroy us financially.

I tried to intervene. I shut off her debit cards and credit cards; this only enraged her; Crystal demanded money to shop. I attempted to give her a generous monthly allowance, but this only pissed her off. I knew it was an addiction, but I did not realize **IT WAS A SYMPTOM OF DEPRESSION**. We lost our savings for a down payment on a home. The credit that I worked so hard to build was being destroyed. Eventually, her dream car, the BMW Z4 Roadster, had to be voluntarily surrendered. Due to her excessive spending, I could not keep up with the vehicle's necessary maintenance, and the transmission malfunctioned. I could not afford to replace the $6,000 transmission, so I called the bank and requested a voluntary surrender, which further destroyed my credit. I was frustrated but not angry, sad, but not angry.

More importantly, during her spending spree, no money was being spent on the supplements that kept her calm. The anger and rage returned with a vengeance. She began to lash out at me once again, blaming me for everything. I went online and found another car, but with damaged credit, we were now paying $526 for a car payment instead of the $280 for the BMW. I didn't engage in arguments with my wife. I just began to look for a second job. Eventually, I found one, but Crystal was unhappy with the second job I found as a bus driver. I would be driving college students to and from their apartment complex to the college campus. **It triggered** all of her hurtful memories of when I was working as a bus driver for the City of Fresno. During a portion of that time, I was very unfaithful. So she began to lash out at me for that as well. It started all over again, the yelling, the screaming, and the cussing. This time not only was she demanding a divorce, but she began to look for another place to live. I knew something else was wrong with my wife, but I could not pinpoint the problem.

It was now late 2017. Crystal had mellowed out again. The wave of tyranny had paused. She decided that she wanted to go back to school and work on her education. I thought it was great. I told her I was very proud of her. During the chaos many years earlier, I was able to get my wife approved for SSI Disability due to her mental illness. The department of rehab had partnered with SSI to help recipients go back to school, get an education, and get back into the workforce. My wife wanted to take advantage of all there was to offer, so she decided to go this route. It was a decision that we both regretted. (My wife will explain in her book) I contacted SSI and the department of Rehab and got her registered with the program and registered for college. I went shopping and got all her school supplies. She was excited, and I was excited for her. I wish we only knew what was about to transpire.

THE BREAK

In January of 2018, Crystal started college. She was excited, but things did not go as planned. During her second semester, an incident transpired at the college that uprooted and triggered her childhood trauma. One of her male college professors asked her for sex and when Crystal refused, he treated her like shit for the entire semester.

The reason why this was triggering for Crystal was that she had been concealing a secret. Something she never chose to talk about or seek therapy for. Crystal had been repeatedly molested, raped, and beaten by both her uncle and her mother's boyfriend during her childhood. This deplorable, sick abuse had gone on for many years, from late elementary through late junior high school. Crystal told her mother, but her mother did nothing, allowing the abuse to continue. I found all of this out after the events that would unfold after her second semester ended.

I need to say this...

Finding out about my wife's tragic childhood broke my heart and it made me take a hard look at myself and how I treated her in the past. My wife had been tragically broken before we met, and here I come, a broken man, with my unresolved pain and hurts, and add to her anguish, damaging her further. During the early part of our relationship, I had compounded her pain immeasurably. Crystal had been suffering in silence since childhood. Now her suffering would become uncontrollable as she slowly began to lose control of reality.

BIPOLAR? OR JUST IN PAIN?

◆•————————•————————•◆

I n mid-2019, my wife began to have these panic attacks. They were mild at first, shortness of breath, along with a little pain in her chest. She would get these from time to time. It seemed like once every couple of months. I asked her if she needed to go to the doctor, but she refused, saying that she would be okay. She began to attack me verbally again. However, this time she was relentless. The attacks of shouting, screaming, and cursing became more frequent and more intense. She began to fight with me repeatedly about the past, as though we never discussed it. She started accusing me of cheating again. She was convinced that I was seeing other women. No matter how hard I tried to convince her I was not, it did not work. Her mind was made up. I would leave the apartment and sit outside in the car, to give her some space. I did not understand what was happening. After a couple of hours of being outside, I would try to come into the apartment, but she had locked me out. I would ring the doorbell, figuring she locked the door by accident, only to have her come to the door and tell me, "Get the fuck out of here! You no longer live here! Go back to that bitch's house that you were at!" I would just turn and go back to the garage. A few hours later, she would come outside and kick the garage door. I would open it, and she would come in filled with rage. She would yell, "You think you are slick sitting out here in the garage? I know what you are up to. I know you are talking on the phone with your other bitch. You think I'm stupid, fuck you! I fucking hate you!"

These attacks went on for hours at a time, for days and weeks at a time. A typical fit of rage would last when I got home from work at 3:50 pm and would end about 2-3 am. My wife was relentless. She would argue with me until she was exhausted. Then it would stop. Just as quickly as it started, it would stop. Crystal would burst into tears and apologize. Of course, I would forgive her and tell her, "I accept your apology," but I knew something was wrong.

I found an African American male therapist for us to talk with. He was married to a white woman. During our first session, Crystal asked him, "How can you understand a black woman if you are not committed to one?" He assured Crystal that he could help, but he could not. Not primarily because of his "Therapeutic approach" (that was part of it) but because my wife's mental state was way passed the "Therapy" stage at that point.

I decided to end our therapy sessions with the African American therapist after a one-on-one session I had with him. During our session, he asked me if I knew why my wife was still treating me in such a horrible fashion. I told him I was not sure. I told him I was split between two thoughts. I said, "Obviously she is still hurt for the ways I treated her in the past, but I don't know why she attacks me like it just happened." The therapist asked me, "How many years have passed since you have become this changed man?" I said, "11 years." He said, "Okay, I understand your thought. It has been quite some time. What is your other thought?" I said, "I don't think my wife knows what it is like to be alone." The therapist asked, "What do you mean?" I said, "Every time my wife has been hospitalized, I was faced with the fact of being alone. I've spent weeks and weeks, month after month, without her at home. I've had to struggle with thoughts that she might not return and I might not get to hold her again. I've got a taste of what life is like without the person I love; it hurts. I don't think Crystal understands that feeling because, despite the way she has been treating me, I have not left." The therapist replied, "Well maybe you should leave. Maybe you should give her a taste of her own medicine. Maybe she needs to know what it feels like without you at home. Can you afford to find a place of your own?"

I was stunned at his response. I said, "No, I can't afford a place of my own and I would not try to leave or move out." He asked, "Why not? That is no way to live." I said, "Because I love my wife and I made her a promise." The therapist just sat there for a second thinking about what I said and then he replied, "Well, I think you should give it some more thought; you don't deserve to go through what she is putting you through. You don't deserve to live that way." Our session ended and he said he would have his secretary call me to schedule another appointment. When his secretary called, I informed her that we would no longer be seeing him as our therapist.

I took Crystal to see another therapist in town. This time a white man with over 25 years of experience. He was an asshole to my wife. During our first session, he began to antagonize Crystal asking her, "What is your problem? Why are you acting this way? Are you a child or an adult?" I had to intervene and remind him that we were there because she was having problems with forgiving me for the ways I had treated her. Crystal completely shut down and refused to speak to him for the remainder of our visit.

On our second visit with this therapist, the first question he asked Crystal was, "How old are you?" she replied, "I'm 53." He asked her, "Are you still able to have an orgasm?" We both looked at him in shock and Crystal asked, "Why are you asking me that?" He said, "I'm just wondering how your sex life is and if you still enjoy having sex with your husband." Crystal answered, "Yes and yes." He said, "Okay, that is good. Do you have oral sex? Do you swallow?" I mumbled out, "What the fuck?" Crystal looked at me and then looked at him and asked, "What is up with these questions?" I asked, "Yeah, what does that have to do with anything?"

The therapist replied, "I'm just wondering how far you both go to please each other during sex." I became upset and I replied, "It seems like you are only interested in what she does, but you have not asked me whether I eat pussy or not." Crystal looked at me and laughed. The therapist had this uncomfortable look as his face turned bright red. He was quiet for a moment then he said, "Well I think that is enough for today."

Crystal and I got up to leave. I shook hands with the therapist and thanked him for his time. I told him we would no longer be needing his services. I went online to find other therapists, psychologists, and psychiatrists, but they were out of our budget. Charging over $200 for the first visit and around $150-$195 for each follow-up. If I knew then what I know now, I would have said, "The hell with our bills," and paid those fees.

Crystal also suffered from a bone disease called Paget's disease of the bone. She was diagnosed with this disease in 2013. It is a disease that affects how her bones grow. Our bones are constantly breaking down and re-growing. The bones don't grow in length, but they grow in thickness and strength. Paget's disease causes this process to happen faster than average. So the bones grow more quickly than expected and are not strong. Due to this accelerated growth, it causes pain in the joints. Crystal also suffered from arthritis in her lower spine. So, she had already been battling physical pain, and now, her mental health was beginning to decline. She did not want to get back on pharmaceuticals, so we decided to see a different type of doctor and get her approved for a Medical Marijuana card. My wife began to try cannabis for her pain. Huge Mistake!

DYING IN MY ARMS

◆—————————●——————————◆

W e started to buy marijuana from a trusted source, and it was working -at first. Crystal was calm; her physical pain had gone away, and her mood and spirit had lifted. She was laughing and smiling again. It was great for about a month, and then she started to have horrible panic attacks and hallucinations. I know you are probably thinking she smoked too much, or we got a bad batch. No! I smoked with her. I would learn the following year that my wife had begun to hallucinate. She had been suffering **auditory hallucinations all along, a symptom of PTSD**. She had never been previously diagnosed. We would not learn about this diagnosis until a year later in 2020. I will go into more detail later in the book.

In May of 2019, she suffered two panic attacks within a couple of days. The first one was so severe, that she stopped breathing. I was in the kitchen, Crystal was in the dining room, and we were talking while I was washing dishes. She stood up and walked over to me at the sink and said, "I don't feel right, I'm scared, can you hold me?" She did not look good. I dropped the dishes and rushed over to her. As I held her, her body began to take in and expel air in the scariest, most unnatural way. It was like she was not getting enough oxygen. Her breathing became extremely labored, sucking in vast amounts of air and then forcefully expelling the air out. I remember telling her, "Babe talk to me, tell me what's going on." Her head went back as she was beginning to lose consciousness, but her breathing was still labored and her eyes were open. I shook her gently as I called her name. When she did not respond, I shook her a little more, asking if she could hear me. Then she stopped breathing. I felt her stomach, her diaphragm, against my stomach, push out her last breath. I looked at her. I felt her go limp. Her eyes were open, her mouth was open, and her head had fallen back. I began to panic as I shouted at her, "Babe! Baby! Baby, can you hear me?"

Crystal gave no response, and she was still not breathing. I laid her down on the kitchen floor. I was panicking, and shouting, "No! No! No!" I grabbed the cordless phone and called 911. I was crying as I told the dispatcher my wife stopped breathing. I remember being unable to stop staring into my wife's empty eyes. It felt like I was floating over our bodies like I was watching us. The dispatcher was asking me all of the necessary questions. I answered her the best I could. She told me an ambulance was on the way and not to hang up.

I interlocked my fingers and placed the palm of my hands on my wife's chest; I cried out, "Please!" as I pushed down on her chest. Then, for a split second, I went blank. It was as if time stopped. I don't remember anything except staring into Crystal's eyes as my tears fell onto her face. It was the last thing I remember, but also the first thing I remember when I came back to consciousness. It only lasted a split second. Then her eyes fluttered. She began to gasp, and then take very shallow breaths, but she was breathing gradually! I remember shouting at the dispatcher, "My wife is breathing! My wife is breathing!"

Crystal began to move her eyes, trying to look around. Then she asked me why she was on the kitchen floor. I had the dispatcher on speakerphone, so I told Crystal, "Babe, it is okay, just relax." The dispatcher began to ask me something when Crystal interrupted and said, "I'm okay I'm just a little embarrassed." The dispatcher asked me who was that talking in the background. I told her, "It's my wife."

The dispatcher began to ask Crystal her name, age, place of birth, etc. The ambulance arrived, and I let the paramedics in. I helped them pick Crystal up off the floor and into a chair. They checked all her vitals as I explained what had taken place. They were surprised yet confused because her vitals were normal. They asked Crystal if she wanted to go to the hospital, but she refused. I suggested that she go. I told the paramedics to take her, but I could not make Crystal go. They made it clear to me that it was her decision. Crystal was more embarrassed than afraid. She said she felt fine. I asked if she was sure, and she said yes. The paramedics told us that they were glad that she felt okay. They had Crystal sign a waiver and they left.

Three days later, Crystal suffered another panic attack that left her unable to walk. She felt like she was suffering a heart attack. Crystal was taken to the hospital emergency room via ambulance. I rode with her, scared, crying, holding her hand. She was in the hospital for hours. The doctors ruled it a "**Panic attack due to social stressors.**" What transpired at the college the year before **triggered her past** in a way we could never imagine.

PSYCHOSIS, THE FIRST TIME CRYSTAL GOES MISSING

In June of 2019, Crystal was in pain again. She smoked some cannabis, and after a few minutes, her pain was gone. She was calm, but then she went to the freezer and put food into a paper bag. I asked her what she was doing, and she said, "I have a surprise, get dressed." She began to empty all of the contents of the freezer into the bag. I asked her again, "Babe, what are you doing?" I tried to reach into the bag to put the food back, and she snapped at me, "Don't touch that! Put it back!" I did not want to trigger another argument, so I left the food alone, went to our room, and got dressed. I returned to the kitchen, and Crystal began to put the bags of frozen food into the car. She said, "Get in; we are taking a trip." I asked where we were going. She said, "It's a surprise."

Now clearly, Crystal was in no condition to drive. So I just remained calm and was able to talk and take the keys out of her hands. I told her, "That's a fine babe. I will drive, and you can tell me where to turn. You just smoked some weed, and you don't seem able to get us there safe."

She agreed and got in the car. She told me to get on the freeway like I was going to work. As we got onto the freeway, she began to talk to herself. She was staring out of the passenger window and having a full conversation. I could not hear her because she was only "Mouthing" the words and not verbally speaking. I tried to ask her where we were going (doing 65mph during rush hour traffic at 5:30 pm), but she just held up one finger, signaling me not to interrupt her while talking. I tried to ask her again, and she looked at me and yelled, "Wait!" I could see something was wrong, so I got off at the next exit and got back onto the freeway heading home. After a few minutes, she realized what I was doing and became irate.

Crystal shouted at me, "You're blowing the surprise. Your cousin Joe rented us a room for our honeymoon." I just looked at her. Crystal was talking…but it was not her. I told her, "Baby, we got married 14 years ago." She had this confused look on her face like she was trying to process what I was saying. She just shook her head, stared out of the window, and began talking to herself again. I raced home. When we arrived, we both got out of the car and began to walk to the front door. I was watching Crystal the entire time. We were standing on the porch, and as I unlocked the door, Crystal began to panic. She said she did not feel right. I asked if she wanted to sit down, and she nodded. I sat her down on the porch. I asked her if she wanted some water, and she said, "Yes."

I rushed inside, grabbed a glass, and poured some water, but as soon as I rushed back outside, she was gone! I looked at the car and said, "Babe?" All of our windows are tinted, so it is hard to see inside. So I walked up to the car and opened the door. She was not inside. I began to panic. I yelled out, "Babe!" I ran to the right side of our condo, looked over the back fence, and yelled, "BABE!" She was not back there. I looked down our driveway; I did not see her. I noticed the neighbor's side gate was open. I ran into their backyard, hoping to find her, but she was not there, and the neighbors were not home.

I ran down to the edge of our driveway and looked down both sides of the street. I did not see her. We lived in a cul-de-sac, so I ran to the end of the block thinking to myself, she could not have gone that far. I was only inside for a split second. I ran in and out of the yards of the other condos on both sides of the street. She was not on our block. I ran down every block in our neighborhood, in and out of the yards, looking over fences and yelling out, "Crystal! Babe! Babe!" She was not in our area. I ran back to our home. I got in the car and began to think back to the years 2011-2012.

When Crystal would get upset and leave on foot, she had this "Route" she would walk. I drove that route, but she was not walking there. We live off a busy main street. On that main street are stores like Wal-Mart, WinCo, and CVS Pharmacy. I drove through each parking lot and got out of the car to look for her. I ran in and out of each store, but I did not find her. **I wanted to call the police, but I'm black. We are black. That was the last resort**. I left the store, worried. It was getting dark. I was trying to remain calm so I could think. We live around the corner from an elementary school, and behind that elementary school is a park. I drove to the park, and their Crystal was, sitting on a bench.

Crystal's hair was not combed, and she was not wearing any makeup. (Not that she needed any) She was wearing her pajamas, which consisted of very sheer, tight, black yoga-like pants, a white button-up front half shirt with four buttons. Only two of the bottom buttons were fastened. She was not wearing a bra, so her boobs were pretty noticeable, and there was a group of guys on the field in front of her playing soccer. I pulled up, parked the car, and yelled, "Babe!" I quickly walked toward her. She was talking on her cell phone. I said, "Babe, what are you doing here? Who are you talking to?" (She took her cellphone, I never thought to call it, and 45 minutes had passed.) I was relieved to find her, but I immediately became furious with frustration. I said, "C'mon babe, let's go home." She said, "I don't want to; I'm fine." I said, "Babe, I've been looking for you this whole time. Why did you leave?" She said, "I felt like going for a walk." She was still talking to someone on the phone, so I asked her again, "Who are you talking to?" She ignored me and kept on talking. I tried to snatch the phone from her but was unsuccessful. She grabbed the phone with both hands and began to pull, shouting, "What's wrong with you? I told you I'm fine!"

I caught myself and let go of the phone. She began to talk to whomever she was talking to again like nothing was going on. I took a deep breath and said, "Babe, you are not okay. You just left, not telling me anything; I've been looking for you for almost an hour. Look at the way you are dressed right now. It is not safe for you to be outside like this." Crystal looked down at herself and yelled, "Fine! I will walk home!" I said, "Babe, you can't walk around outside like this. Get in the car." She said, "No, I want to walk." She began to walk home, so I got into the car and followed her, driving slowly along the curb. Cars with guys were driving by slow, honking, asking her if she needed a ride. A guy pulled up behind me and honked the horn. The dude yelled, "A baby!" I parked the car and got out. As I walked toward my wife, the guy drove off.

I said, "C'mon babe, I will take you the rest of the way home." She told whoever she was speaking to on the phone to hold on. She put the phone to her side and said, "I'm not getting in the car; I told you I'm walking home," Then she turned around, confused, and began to walk back to the park. I lost my composure. I walked up behind her and snatched the phone out of her hand, I looked at the phone to see who she was talking to and…she was talking to no one. There was no active phone call; her phone was on the home screen. She immediately became filled with rage. I took her phone and snapped it in half, handed it back to her, and yelled, "Now get in the fucking car!"

You guys are probably thinking, why not leave and let her walk home? Here is why. Number one: she is not in her right frame of mind, and number two: months earlier, a jogger was jogging down the street several blocks away. They spotted the dead naked body of an African American woman, thrown into the corner. She had been sexually assaulted and then strangled. They never caught the suspect. Whoever did that was still out there… Meanwhile, I was not going to take any chances with Crystal's life.

Crystal's mood immediately changed; she became calm. She asked me for my phone. I asked her why. She told me she was talking to her daughter earlier and wanted to let her know that she was okay. I thought to myself, *"your daughter?" But there was no one on the phone. She had not spoken to either one of her daughters in years and for a good reason.* I asked her, "Which daughter are you referring to?" She said, "My oldest." I gave her my phone; however, she proceeded to call my cousin Joe, and she had still not gotten into the car. She began walking on the sidewalk, so I got into the car, and I began to follow her. She hung up with my cousin and called a good friend that I work with. Her conversation with both of these individuals was very bizarre. She was not making any sense at all.

We got to our driveway and I drove up and parked in front of our place. Crystal was standing down at the edge of the driveway, looking out into the street. She was no longer talking on the phone; she was just standing, watching traffic go by. I walked down to her and said, "C'mon babe, let's get you inside." She said, "I'm not going into the apartment." I asked, "Why not?" She said, "Because I don't have to." She turned around and began to walk quickly down the sidewalk toward the street. I jumped in front of her walking backward while trying to block her path. I said, "Babe, talk to me, tell me why you don't want to go inside." She started to become angry again and yelled, "I don't have to explain anything to you; you are not my father!" and she shoved me backward out of her way. I lost my balance and fell backward. I quickly got to my feet and chased after her.

By this time, we had made it to the edge of the street. We were standing at the curb on the grass. There were four lanes of traffic. Two lanes go north, and two lanes go south. She tried to run around me and into traffic as she yelled, "Leave me alone, and move!" I managed to grab her shirt and pull her back to the curb. She squatted down, trying to pull herself out of my grip. She began to yell for help, demanding that I let her go. She began to hit my wrists, trying to free herself. I started to panic. If her shirt would have ripped or I lost my grip, she would end up falling into the street and getting hit by northbound traffic.

I pulled her towards me. I managed to get my arms around her. She was squirming hard, trying to free herself from my grip. She was screaming for help, and I could hear car horns honking as they drove by. I was losing my grip. Crystal managed to free one arm and began to hammer her fist at my face. I was able to wrap my arms around her body. I picked her up off the ground and carried her back down the block. I tried to calm her down, but she was furious. She was kicking me and squirming around as I carried her. She managed to free her arms and began screaming for help. She was pulling my hair, yanking my head backward in the process. I shook my head free, catching a glimpse of her face. Crystal was gone. It was not my wife I was struggling with. I will never forget the look of pure rage and terror on her face. As we got to the apartment, I leaned her up against the wall, pressing my weight against her. I had my right shoulder pinned against her chest. She bit the side of my neck (right trap) in an attempt to free herself. I managed to get the security gate open while she still struggled to get free. By this time, I was in tears and not able to comprehend the full severity of what was taking place or who this woman was. As I flung open the security door, I reached for the front door. Crystal was yelling, "No! No! Stop!"

I managed to slide her along the wall towards the front door, reach the door handle, and push the front door open. She tried to squat down and sit on the front porch. I managed to kneel below her waist and get my shoulder under her (against her stomach like a football tackle) and pick her up. As I carried her inside, she grabbed onto the door frame, yelling and kicking. She was pulling hard at the perimeter, trying to pull us back outside. I pushed hard in the opposite direction. We had a big leather love seat at the front door as you walk in. (A place for Crystal to rest as she took off her shoes when coming from outside). I used my momentum as I leaned inwards, she lost her grip, and we both fell onto the love seat with me on top of her. She yelled, "You fucker!" As she tried to get up and run back outside.

I tried to hurry and shut the front door. It was wide open. So was the security door. I pushed her back down and held her down as I extended my leg, trying to reach the front door with my foot, in an attempt to swing it shut. I closed my eyes and turned my head as she began to punch me in the face again while holding a fist-full of my hair, Crystal was yelling, "I hate you! I fucking hate you!" What I did not realize was that I was choking her. I had my right hand just below her neckline as I pinned her down onto the seat. When I looked at her and realized where my hand was, I froze. I remember staring at her, stuck at the moment. It felt like forever… I will never forget the look of terror on her face as she asked me, "What is wrong with you?" I let her go, and she got up. It was Crystal…she was back. She asked me, "What are you doing? Why would you treat me that way?" She walked out of the front door and to the neighbor's condo. She began to talk to the next-door neighbor. I got on the phone and called her brother. I explained what was happening, and he suggested that I contact the paramedics and get her to the hospital. I apologized to the neighbor as he calmly and patiently listened to my wife explain to him how I had just "beat her up".

I called 911 and requested an ambulance. I explained to the dispatcher that I believe my wife was having an allergic reaction to some marijuana. She said that an ambulance was on the way; I thanked her and hung up. The police showed up a few minutes later.

These two young, unprofessional police officers kept Crystal and me apart. They spent the next 45 minutes trying to get my wife to confess to them that I was beating her. The ambulance came, and the paramedics began to ask my wife questions to "Check her mental status." I could see that Crystal was "In and out" of being herself and this other person. She was refusing to go to the hospital. I tried to walk toward her, telling the officer that she was not well, but he ordered me to stay where I was as he put his hand on his weapon. My wife heard the commotion and decided to go with the paramedics. They took her to the hospital.

The cops refused to tell me what hospital my wife was being transported to. I ended up finding out on my own within that hour. I drove to the hospital and sat outside of the emergency room, not knowing where my wife was located. About 10 minutes later, she came walking out. I stood up and began to walk to her. The security staff tried to get her to go back into the hospital to check in, but she refused.

I tried to get her to check in as well. I was telling her that she needed help. She told me she wanted to go to the Marjaree Mason Center, a place for battered and abused women. I was confused, and asked her why. I pleaded with her to see a doctor, but she said she was not going into the hospital. So I took her to the battered women's shelter, but they refused to allow her to stay since she had not been a victim of domestic violence. They let her go, and I took her home. Crystal still refused to go inside the apartment. She said she was scared but did not know why. I told her that it was ok. We slept outside, in the car. This event started at around 6 pm on Friday. It was now 4 am Saturday.

I asked my wife months later what changed her mind about going to the hospital that night. She said, "I can remember looking over at you and seeing how the cops were treating you. I knew that if I went to the hospital, they would have to leave since I was the reason they were there. I was scared they were going to kill you. So I told the lady paramedic, "I'm scared for my husband's life; I will go to the hospital.""

FINDING HELP

The next couple of months kind of flew by. In August, my wife flew out to see her daughter in Kansas (a huge, huge mistake). When she returned, we celebrated her birthday. I watched her closely. She was still arguing with me, but now her new piece of ammunition was how I was "Choking her" that night. I tried to explain the situation to her, but all she remembered was being at the park, and then I was choking her. I knew something was wrong because she could not remember the details of that evening. I just blamed it on the marijuana to avoid an argument. September and October were pretty much the same; she was still yelling and lashing out. Crystal had become afraid of sleeping in the bedroom, so we had been sleeping in the living room on a blown-up bed. I asked her if she knew why she was afraid of sleeping in the room. She told me she was scared someone was going to get her. I reassured her that she was safe and that I would not let anything happen to her. She just looked at me and put her head down. I had gotten pretty good at maintaining my composure once again; however, I still spent much time outside, in the car, and the garage.

November and December came around. I tried to keep things as normal as possible. Crystal had become immersed in one of her daughter's failing careers and relationships. That was cool with me because it kept her mind occupied with someone other than myself. She had a new person in her crosshairs, and I was just glad for the time being that it was not me.

During the "downtime" I managed to find two remarkably loving, insightful and understanding psychologists for my wife and me to speak with. **Dr. Kelly Horton** and **Dr. Marchita (pronounced Markeeta) Masters**. During the chaos, I never stopped seeking help for my wife. It took a while because there were not a lot of black women therapists in our area. And definitely, not a lot of black women psychologists in our area either. I found both women through my health insurance benefits. **Dr. Horton was in the bay area**, and **Dr. Masters was in San Diego**. We started seeing them online via video-health visits. Dr. Horton saw my wife and me together for couple's therapy, and Dr. Masters saw my wife and me separately. Words can't begin to describe these two women. Their level of experience, concern, compassion, counsel, and empathy were both irreplaceable and invaluable. My wife and I will be forever grateful to both of these women.

My wife and I were in session with Dr. Horton in late 2019. Dr. Horton witnessed one of my wife's horrible, hate-filled angry tirades for the first time. Crystal sat there for the entire 50min session and let me have it with both barrels. I was embarrassed, but I dealt with it. On December 31, 2019, I was in session with Dr. Masters. It was an eye-opening, powerful therapy session. For the first time, Dr. Masters helped me realize…I mean really understand, what I had put my wife through. **I knew what I had done and what I had been; however, I did not realize it from an abused woman's "Psychological perspective**."

Dr. Master's also shared a very powerful yet insightful message; she said, "Children are like sponges, soaking up whatever behaviors are prevalent in their environment. Your childhood and teenage environment were filled with hate, destruction, and violence, and although you are a changed man, and no longer possess those traits, your wife's emotional injuries are still very fresh in her mind with your past abusive behavior." Dr. Masters helped me really understand, unconsciously I had taken on the characteristics of my abusers.

The session was overwhelming. I sat at the table and cried for about 20 minutes after our session ended. Crystal was in the kitchen. I walked over to her and apologized once again for all of my past behavior. The last thing I remember was hugging her, and then everything went black.

TAKING ITS TOLL

◆———————●———————◆

I woke up minutes later on the kitchen floor. I remember a vision of Crystal over me crying on the phone. Then everything went black again. The next thing I remember was waking up to a paramedic kneeling over me, trying to ask me questions. I was lying on the kitchen floor and Crystal had propped a pillow under my head. The paramedics helped me off the floor and helped me sit down in the dining room. They checked my vitals and my blood sugar as they asked me questions as to what had taken place.

I did not mention to you, the reader, that I had been wearing a heart monitor earlier that year. I had been wearing one for about six weeks. Along with my doctor, I was trying to figure out why I was having these horrible chest pains, shortness of breath, palpitations, dizzy spells, and loss of balance from time to time. There were times when I almost passed out and fell off the toilet when taking a dump, and I began to see bright flashes of light along with worsening blurred vision. My father died in his early 50's. He had a stroke and then died of an aneurism. I was scared that I was going down that same path.

Do you remember earlier in this book when I mentioned I had gotten a second job? I got that job in 2017 and did not quit until Feb 2019. This entire time I was trying to help my wife while working two jobs. I worked 40hrs a week at my day job and one point, 30hrs per week on my second job. For about three months, I was working 70hrs per week. I worked from 7 am to 3:30 pm Monday-Friday and then 4 pm to 10 pm at my part-time job. Then the 70 hours went down to 58 hours and then down to 52 hours. I eventually quit that job in Feb. of 2019, but the damage had already been done. You see, to stay awake at my second job and stay up all night to help my wife, I was drinking four Red Bulls a day before I got off work at 3:30 pm. Then while on my second job, I would drink another two Red Bulls at around 8 pm. This would help me make it to 10 pm and stay awake to keep an eye on my wife. I did this for over a year, and it, along with the stress, was finally taking its toll.

PSYCHOSIS, THE SECOND TIME CRYSTAL GOES MISSING

◆━━━━━━●━━━━━━◆

January 2020 was when things had taken a turn for the worst. My wife had begun to accuse me of cheating again. She became more verbally abusive. As usual, I just let her vent until she tired herself out, and then I would apologize and try to keep it moving. We were still seeing Dr. Horton and Dr. Masters, but my wife's condition was becoming worse. She was now sleeping all day and being wide awake full of energy at night, so she could be sure to let me have it. I added Monsters and Rock Star drinks to my arsenal to stay awake.

My wife came to me in the middle of January. With this story…

"I got out of the shower today and as I opened the bathroom window to let the steam out, I heard two guys talking outside the window. They were talking about you and this apartment. They discussed all of the different women you had running in and out of here while I was gone. One of the guys said, "Isn't he married?" The other guy said, "Yeah, but his wife is out of town in Kansas visiting her daughter." They said that you had women in and out of here all night, every night. As I said, James, you are a sorry mutha-fucka. You have not changed one bit. You are the same old James, you just got better at playing your games, and I am a stupid bitch for believing in you."

I could not believe what I was hearing. It was total bullshit, so I asked, "Oh yeah? Who are these guys?" She said, "The neighbors." I said, "Ok, I'm going over there and ring the doorbell and ask them to come over here." I turned and left the bathroom. Before I could get to the front door, she ran in front of me and pressed her back against the door, and said, "Wait." I told her to get out of the way. She asked me, "What are you going to do." I said, "I'm going to ask the neighbor to come over here so I can hear this from his mouth, and when I beat the fuck out of him for lying, I'm going to ask you to repeat what you heard him say." She said, "Wait! Don't! I don't know who it was." I asked, "What do you mean?" She said, **"I could not see who was talking."** I asked, "What are you talking about?" Crystal had this confused look on her face. She said, **"I don't know who said it, but that's what I heard. I could not see them, but it was two guys talking outside the window."**

In my next session with Dr. Horton, I told her this story. She said, "It sounds like your wife's mental health is declining. **It sounds like she was hallucinating. It is not uncommon for people that have PTSD or who have been under that amount of stress, for that amount of time, to start hallucinating."** She suggested that I get my wife into a hospital.

I was devastated, but it all made sense as I thought back to my wife's erratic behavior. I went to my wife and suggested that we take her to the hospital to get checked out. Of course, she became upset and refused. She felt like I was using the hospital as an excuse to get rid of her so that I could continue to cheat. I explained to her that it was Dr. Horton's suggestion. She asked if I told the doctor what she said. I told her, yes, and she became furious; she began to cuss me out again. I just left the apartment and went outside to the car. She locked the door behind me. She came outside about every 30 to 40 minutes to bang on the door and window while shouting and cussing me out. I made up my mind at that moment that I had enough of this life. I was beginning to feel like giving up, like I no longer wanted to live. It was a Friday evening. On Monday, I was going to file for divorce.

I woke up Saturday morning. I had to use the bathroom. The neighbors were outside, so I could not pee on the side of the fence as I had done before. I was not in the garage where I left my pee containers, and the remote to open the garage was in the apartment. I went to the front door and rang the doorbell, but there was no answer. I got my keys to unlock the door expecting the security chain to be on, but it was off. I was able to walk in and use the bathroom.

Crystal must have woken up because she called my name and asked me to come into the living room. I went to where she was and stood there. She was lying down on the blow-up bed. She asked me to lie down next to her, but I refused. She began to cry. She apologized once again for how she had treated me, but I heard it all before. I stopped her from speaking, and I said, "I'm going to file for divorce on Monday. Thirteen years have gone by. I'm not the same man, but you can't forgive me, and no matter what I do, you seem to be very unhappy. I want you to be happy. You will only be satisfied with me out of your life. So I'm leaving."

Crystal began to cry profusely. It hurt me to see her in pain. However, the stress was taking a toll on my health. I could not continue this way and I wanted to be happy. I turned to leave, and she cried out loud, "Please don't leave me." She was holding her face in her hands and crying uncontrollably. She said, "I'm sorry, I don't know what is wrong with me. I need your help."

I stood there for a second. I did not know what to say. What do I do? Do I think about my own mental and physical health and leave? Or do I stay to try and help my wife and continue to be abused?

I told her I need to think about what she just said. She asked why. I said, "Because I made up my mind yesterday to leave you. I did not expect to hear this from you this morning. Now I have to think about what I'm going to do." I turned and left to go back outside. She began to cry again. I sat outside for about 20 minutes, not knowing what to do; I was torn. I came back inside, and Crystal was still lying down in the living room. I took off my jacket and shoes and lay down next to her. I put my arms around her and kissed her forehead. She began to cry. I told her we need to get her some serious help, and she agreed. After a few minutes, she asked me what changed my mind. I told her, "I still love you, and I can't leave you like this. We need to get you some help. We need to figure out what is going on. We need to make sure you are ok." She was quiet for a minute and then got up and went to the bathroom.

Crystal came out a few minutes later, fully dressed with her car keys and purse. I asked her what she was doing, and she said she needed to go for a walk. I got up to go with her, but she told me she wanted to go alone. She told me she needed some time to think. I asked her, "about what?" She shouted, "Didn't you take some time out for yourself to think this morning?" I could hear her tone begin to change. I said, "Ok, ok. No problem. We will talk when you get back." I walked her to the door and watched her leave. I stood in the doorway as I always did to blow her a kiss goodbye, but instead of blowing me a kiss back, she yelled out, "Go and get the phone. I will call you."

I walked to the kitchen and began to wash dishes. About 1 minute later, the phone rang. I answered the phone, and this is what my wife had to say:

"I wrote you a letter. When we hang up, I want you to read it. I put the letter in the compartment where we keep the remote control to the T.V. I know that you have been cheating on me, and I know who you have been cheating on me with. Before I left to go out of town to visit my daughter, I hired a private investigator. This investigator watched you the entire time I was gone. He told me about the women that you had coming into the apartment. I know when you went to the car this morning after our talk, it was not so that you could think. I know you called that other bitch and told her that you changed your mind about leaving me. While you were outside, I called the police to let them know that I was leaving you. I let them know not to come after you. I told them that no "Foul play" was involved, and this was my choice. (I tried to interrupt to ask her what was going on, but it did not work) I'm not going for a walk this morning; I'm leaving you. I don't know where I'm going. I have no money, no family, and no place to go. I'm parking the car down Huntington (Blvd). It will be next to our favorite tree. I'm leaving my purse, wallet, car keys, and cell phone in the backseat. I won't be needing them. Now you can be with your other bitch. I won't bother you guys. I want you both to be happy. Now call your bitch to come and pick you up and bring you to pick up the car. Goodbye, James." Crystal hung up.

I yelled out, "Fuck!" And threw the cordless phone against the wall. I hurried and put on my shoes, grabbed my keys, and took off for Huntington...On foot! I ran and jogged the entire 3 miles. I was exhausted as I reached the car. I looked inside, hoping to find her sitting there, but she was not. Her purse, wallet, and keys were in the backseat, along with her cell phone. I got her phone and checked her call logs and voicemails, trying to find a clue as to where she might have gone. There was a voicemail from Fresno P.D. An officer attempted to contact her to talk about the "Situation with her husband." He left his name and number.

I tried to call back but was unsuccessful in reaching him. I drove around for hours, thinking of where she could be. I checked the train station and the Poverello House which is a homeless shelter. I drove up and down Huntington. I called the Marjoree Mason center, but that was a dead end. I called the hospitals to see if she had checked herself in but that was a dead end as well. I went through her call logs and saw that she contacted her daughter, the one who lived in Kansas. So I hit redial. Her daughter answered, and I told her that her mother was missing and began to explain the situation. Her daughter was a jerk and no help at all. I reminded her of the conversation I had with her five months prior regarding her mother's erratic behavior, bone disease, and mental health. (Her daughter visited me at our condo along with her boyfriend). I told her that her mother was now missing. Her daughter did not care. She chuckled as she proceeded to chastise me over the phone, sarcastically saying, "Wow, you're her husband, and you don't even know where your wife is? What a fucking loser. Well, I don't know where she is, and even if I did, I wouldn't fucking tell you." Then Crystal's cell phone went dead.

Hours had gone by. I called Crystal's cousin and brother to see if Crystal had contacted them, but they had not heard from her. I explained the situation to each of them. Her cousin left her house to help look for Crystal as I returned home to see if she had come back. I got to the apartment, but she was not there. I sat at the table and cried. Then I prayed for Crystal; I prayed for her safe return. Then I called the police department to file a missing person report.

I was on the phone with P.D, speaking with a polite female dispatcher. I was explaining the situation to her when the doorbell rang. I got up and opened the door…it was Crystal! I began to cry as I told the police dispatcher that my wife had returned and that she was ok. The dispatcher was happy, and we hung up the call. But something was wrong. Something was terribly wrong.

Crystal just stood at the door; she was not moving. I grabbed her coat and pulled her in. I could not stop crying as I held her tight, asking her to please talk to me. She just stood there. I asked her how she got home, but she did not answer. I let her go and then looked at her as I held her face and asked her, "Where did you go?" Her face was ice-cold and so were her hands. It was apparent that wherever she had been, she was outside the entire time.

TINA

I looked at her face, and her expression was blank. I looked into her eyes as I called her name; everything was empty, no life. I said, "Come on, babe, come in and sit down." She reluctantly came inside. I took off her coat, and I looked her over, making sure that she was okay. There were no torn clothes, scrapes, bruises, or scratches. I saw that her slippers were dirty and dusty. It's like she had been walking. I sat her down on the couch, went to turn on the heater, and then into the kitchen to turn on our Keurig to make her a cup of tea. I came back and sat down in front of her on the floor as I took off her dirty slippers and this was our conversation:

Crystal said, "Don't fucking touch me." I said, "Babe? What are…?"

She interrupted, "I'm not your fucking babe. That weak bitch is not here. That worthless bitch is gone."

I asked, "What do you mean? What are you talking about?"

She said, "You know what I'm talking about. I'm talking about your wife, Crystal; she is pathetic. She is weak and stupid for staying with someone like you. So, I told that weak bitch to leave and not come back, so now I'm here."

I was a little nervous but played it off. I said, "C'mon babe, tell me what's going on."

She said, "Mutha-fucka can't you hear? Are you fucking deaf? And she kicked me in the chest away from her. Didn't I just tell you that I'm not your fucking babe? Mutha-fucka, I am not Crystal. Don't you ever call me, babe." I was kneeling in front of her when she kicked me, so the kick knocked me backward on my ass.

I said, "Ok, who are you?" as I got up.

She said, "I'm Tina. Only I know where Crystal is, so anything you want to say to Crystal, you say it to me, and I will decide whether or not to tell her. No, on second thought, I won't tell her. I don't even want to talk to her because I don't fuck with weak bitches."

I could feel the tears rolling down my cheeks as I realized, once again, that my wife was gone.

I sat there as tears rolled down my face. I stared at Tina as she began to cuss me out, calling me a weak, pathetic mutha-fucking punk. She began to tell me how much of a worthless piece of shit I was for how I had treated Crystal and began to talk about what a stupid, weak bitch Crystal was for never standing up for herself... then; **the doorbell rang, and I saw it. I saw the change**. It was a split second, but it was like it happened in slow motion. That hard, expressionless look on Tina's face left, and suddenly Crystal was back.

The best way I could describe it was as if you were staring at a department store mannequin, and all of a sudden, they blinked.

The doorbell rang again, and this time Crystal turned towards the direction of the front door. She looked worried. I told her it was ok, and I would go and see who it was. I opened the door, and it was her cousin Mae and Crystal's Aunt Marge. They had been driving up and down Huntington and around town looking for her. They asked if I heard anything, and I told them that Crystal had just come home about 15 minutes ago. They were relieved. About 12 hours had passed since I last spoke to her cousin. Crystal's aunt asked if she could see her; I told her that Crystal was not doing very well and wanted to be alone. Then I heard Crystal say, "I'm okay, let them in." They came in and sat next to her, giving her hugs and kisses. Crystal's aunt held her hand and asked her how she was doing. Tears fell from her face as she said, **"Not good; I don't know what's happening to me."** I got up to fix Crystal's tea. I asked her aunt and cousin if they wanted some tea, and they said "Yes," and Crystal's cousin came into the kitchen to make her and her mother some tea. I gave Crystal her tea and sat down. We all talked as I filled them in on what we had been going through. They stayed for a couple of hours as Crystal started to talk about what had taken place when she was a child. I was glad that I had my wife back. But for how long, I did not know.

CRYSTAL'S PTSD FLASHBACK

◆◆———————◆———————◆◆

In January of 2020, my wife started to complain about a sharp pain she was having in the back of her head. She had complained of this pain before. In December of 2019, I had taken her to get a CT scan and some x-rays. The results came back "Normal"; however, she said the pain was getting worse. I asked her what she wanted to do, and she said she wanted to go to the hospital. It was around 11 pm. I jumped up, got my shoes on, and we left. As I was driving up the street, she got her cell phone and began to make a phone call. (I purchased her a new phone) I asked, "Who are you calling?" She said, "My daughter. I want to let her know I'm going to the hospital." Crystal was talking as I got into the left turn lane to get onto the freeway. The light was red, so I was slowing down; she handed me the phone and said, "Here she wants to talk to you." I took the phone, but the light turned green, so I put the phone down as I began to accelerate.

Crystal unlocked her seat belt. I said, "Babe, what are you doing?" She said, "Here, my daughter wants to talk to you," but she had nothing in her hands. I was already committed in the left turn lane. The light was green; I was preparing to get onto the freeway when my wife took off her seatbelt and opened the door, stepping out of the car. I yelled, "Babe! What are you doing?" I grabbed a handful of her jacket as the door flung open at the apex of my left turn. I held on to her jacket, dragging her several feet in the process. I watched the momentum of our forward movement spin my wife's body around, had I let go of her jacket, she would have rolled under our back tire, and I would have run over her head. I stopped the car in the middle of the intersection. I held onto her coat as she yelled, "Let me go!

I struggled with my left hand to put the car into park, turn on the hazard lights and take off my seatbelt because I was stretched out, leaning over the passenger seat while holding onto her coat with my right hand. Cars were zooming past us, going northbound and coming dangerously close to her as they swerved around us to get onto the freeway. I will never forget the look of terror on her face as she looked up at me. She did not know who I was or what was happening. She yelled, "Let me go! Let me go!" I yanked her coat hard, pulling her against the car. She was now seated on the street, facing the rear of the vehicle. I got out and ran around to the passenger side as she struggled to get to her feet. Cars were still flying by us going northbound. I grabbed her coat once again as she tried to run across four lanes of traffic. I leaned back against the car, pulling her hard towards me. I now had a tight grip with both hands on her coat. She was struggling hard to get away, shouting at the top of her lungs, "Help! Help, he is trying to kill me!"

I spun her around, facing me, telling her, "Babe, it is ok, calm down!" She began to hammer her fist at my face, pulling my hair, and yelling, "Let me go!" She accidentally poked my eye with her finger. Out of pure reflex, I let go of her coat with one hand as I reached up to cover my face from her attacks. I could feel myself self-losing my grip on her jacket, so I just closed my eyes and managed to grab hold of her body and spin her around. I was now behind her with my arms wrapped around her, like a bear hug. She began to fling her head back into my face repeatedly. I could start to taste blood in my mouth. I could feel my nose start to bleed. I just held onto her tight as cars drove around us.

Then, I could hear a guy yell out, "Are you ok? Do you need me to call the police?" He was shouting from the sidewalk. Crystal yelled back, "He is trying to kill me!" I looked up; it was a "brotha". He made it across the street and was standing on the median. I looked up and yelled out, "Can you please call for an ambulance? My wife suffers from PTSD. I think she is having a flashback!" He got his cell phone and called for help. Crystal was still struggling to free herself and yelled, "Let me go!" I hugged her tight and said, "Baby, it's me." I managed to trap both of her arms against her chest. I leaned back against the car, pulling her against me. She was now on her tippy-toes, trying to "Jump" herself loose.

Crystal leaned her head back and I was able to position my head alongside hers. I told her, "Baby, it is ok. It is me. I love you; I love you, please stop. It's me, your husband. I'm your husband. You're safe. I'm not going to let anyone hurt you. Please calm down." I could feel her struggle less and less. So, I just kept talking to her. "I love you; I love you. You are safe. No one is going to hurt you." I began to hum a lullaby to her that only she and I knew. It's a lullaby she used to hum when I could not sleep due to being afraid of the dark. (Sid and the closet) I hummed as I held her. I was rocking her slowly from side to side. I could feel her body shaking. After a few seconds, she leaned her head softly against mine. For a minute, it felt like we were the only ones outside. I heard nothing, only my humming. I felt nothing, only my wife's body against mine. Reality quickly set in as the Good Samaritan yelled out, "Help is on the way." I yelled back, "Thank you." He ran back across the street, got into his car, and drove off.

Crystal had calmed down. She was still shaking, and then whispered to me, "I'm hot." She was exhausted, I unzipped her coat, and she was soaking wet with sweat. I told her, "Baby, we need to leave your jacket on. It is cold outside; you are going to be sick." She looked around and asked, "What happened." I rubbed her back as she began to cry. I said, "It's ok. We will talk about it later." She asked, "Why are we in the middle of the street?" I said, "C'mon babe," and sat her down in the car. Crystal was extremely confused, dizzy, and shaking. I noticed the cell phone was still in the groove of the center console. Her daughter never hung up the phone. I grabbed the phone and said, "Hello?" Only it was not her daughter. It was Crystal's friend Cheryl. She had been on the phone the entire time. She told me she heard what was going on and asked if Crystal was ok. I told Cheryl she was fine for now and that I would call her back as soon as I got a chance. She said ok, and we hung up. I called 911 and requested an ambulance. I told the dispatcher, "My wife was diagnosed with PTSD and just suffered a flashback. She needs medical attention." A few minutes later, police officers arrived along with the paramedics.

One of the officers walked over to the passenger side of the car. Crystal was sitting down in the seat, holding her head in her hands. The other officer was talking to the paramedics. The officer asked Crystal, "What's going on." She responded, "Nothing, I just want to go home." The officer said, "I can't let you go home until you tell me what's happened." She said, "I don't know what happened." I told the officer, "My wife suffers from PTSD and just had a flashback." I explained to him what took place and told him I need my wife transported to the hospital. Crystal said, "I'm sorry, I'm ok now, I just want to go home."

The officer ignored the information I gave him and my request to have my wife taken to the hospital. Instead, he said, "Ok, I need to ask you a couple of questions. If you can answer them, you can go." Crystal just put her head down. He asked her how many quarters are in a dollar. She looked up at him but did not answer; she shook her head. The officer said, "I know these questions seem silly, but I have to ask them. If you can answer them, I will let you go home." He asked her the same question again. She still did not respond. He asked her, "Can you tell me who the president of the United States is?" She looked up at him again; only this time, I could see that it was not my wife looking at him. She became agitated and said, "Just take me to the Marjaree Mason center" (the shelter for battered women). The cop asked, "Why? Are you being abused?" Crystal looked up at him again and said, "No, but if you don't let me go home, I want to go there."

Once again I told the officer, "My wife suffers from a mental illness, she has PTSD and just suffered from a flashback. Can we just get her to the hospital?" The officer said it was not up to me to decide whether she went to the hospital. Around this time, he went to talk to his partner, who had just finished talking to the paramedics. The officer came back and said, "Let's get you into the ambulance so they can check you out." Crystal got into the back of the ambulance with both paramedics and the officer. I followed her, trying to talk to one of the paramedics, but he just ignored me. He made sure not to make eye contact with me; he just shut the door in my face as he climbed in.

The other officer said, "Hey, come here, let me talk to you." He asked for my license. I gave it to him, and he called it in. Came back clean (of course), and he then asked me what happened. I told him the whole story. He looked at our car and asked, "Why did you stop almost in the middle of the intersection?" I looked at him and told him, "This is where I stopped as I held onto my wife." He asked, "What do you mean held on to your wife?" I walked back a few feet, frustrated, and pointed to the street. I said, "I dragged my wife from about here, all the way here, as I brought the car to a stop." He looked at our car again. "Lexus?" He said. He walked around the vehicle. "A hybrid?" He looked at me and asked, "What do you do for a living?"

I said, "I work in the automotive industry." He asked, "Where at?" I asked the officer how that information was relevant to what took place this evening. I told him, "My wife needs to be taken to the hospital." He said, "Yeah, yeah, you said she has a mental illness. Has she been diagnosed with one?" I said, "Yes, she has." He asked, "What does she do for a living." I said, "She does not work. She can't right now, she is on SSI Disability for her illness." He just looked at me and asked when she was diagnosed. I said, "Around 2013." He asked, "2013? How long have you guys been together?" I said, "28 years." He looked stunned, "28?" he replied. I just looked at him. At this time, his partner came out of the ambulance and walked over to him. They walked off, so I could not hear what they were saying. I went to the back of the ambulance and knocked on the door. The paramedics never opened the door. I looked through the window and could see the look on Crystal's face. She was gone again.

Both officers walked over to me, and one of them asked, "Do you know why your wife is asking to go to the Marjaree mason center?" I said, "No, I don't." He asked, "Has she been there before?" I said, "No."

He asked sarcastically, "Then how does she know about it?" I replied, "Before her sister was murdered, she was living in the Marjaree mason center." Both officers looked at me. I could see that my response made them feel uncomfortable. They asked when this incident took place. I said, "Years ago, sometime in 1997." The officer replied, "1997?" The other officer told his partner, "They have been together for 28 years." His partner said, "28 years." I said, "Yes, since 1992." He then asked, "You stated your wife suffered a PTSD flashback. Is she a veteran? Was she in the military?" I replied, "No."

They both scoffed as they looked at each other, chuckled, and shook their heads. I told them, "**War veterans are not the only people that suffer from flashbacks or PTSD**." He asked, "Has she been medically diagnosed with a mental illness." I told him, "Yes, she has. I already told your partner." He and his partner walked away again, talking. I walked to the rear of the ambulance and this time I banged on the doors. One paramedic looked out as I asked him to open the door, but he did not. Both officers came back. They walked to the rear of the ambulance, and the paramedic opened the door. Crystal was pissed off. She yelled at me, "Let me have my phone!" I told her, "I will keep your phone for you." She repeated sternly, with her teeth clenched, "Give- me- my- phone, James." I asked the paramedics, "Where are you taking my wife to?" The officers said, "To the hospital."

I gave Crystal's phone to the paramedic, and he handed it to her. I asked them, "As paramedics, wouldn't you want to talk to her husband so you can get a clear understanding of what had taken place? What her medical history is? What she is suffering from? You can look at her and see that she is not well. Why wouldn't you talk to me?" They just ignored me. The officer told them to take her away. I asked the paramedics, "What hospital are you taking my wife to?" They just ignored me. They closed the doors and drove off.

I asked the officers, "What's going on? What hospital is my wife being transported to?" They said they could not tell me. I told them, "This is bullshit. I'm no stranger. I'm her husband." They told me Crystal asked them not to tell me where she was going. I got upset, but I didn't say anything. The officer said I was free to go. I got in my car, got onto the freeway, and sped off, trying to see if I could catch the ambulance, but it was too late. They were gone. It was now around 1 am. I called my wife's cell phone, but my call went straight to voicemail.

PSYCHOSIS, CRYSTAL GOES MISSING A 3RD TIME-CASE # XXXX5385

I drove to every hospital in town, going into each emergency room, giving my wife's name, and asking if she had arrived there. Every hospital told me no one was there by that name. I left upset. I sat in the car for a minute and cried. I was trying to think and trying to keep it together. I called my wife's cell phone, but it still went straight to voicemail. I googled the ambulance company that picked up my wife and managed to find their dispatch number. I called the dispatcher, gave them my wife's name, and asked if they knew what hospital she was taken to. They asked for the location from where she was picked up. I told the dispatcher, "North Peach Ave at the westbound freeway 180 entrance." She looked up the information. She gave me the ambulance vehicle number and told me my wife was taken to Clovis Community Hospital. I thanked her, jumped on the freeway, and drove to the hospital.

I arrived at the emergency room and gave them Crystal's information and asked to see my wife. They looked her up and said they had no patient by that name. They asked what time she was picked up. I looked at the clock; it was now after 3 am. I told them I don't know exactly, but it was a couple of hours ago. They said that it had been a busy Saturday morning. She was probably still waiting in the intake department and had not been checked in yet. I thanked them, went to the emergency waiting room, sat, and waited. I eventually fell asleep. I was exhausted.

I woke up in a panic, a little after 6 am. I called my wife's cell phone; it still went straight to voicemail again. I went back to the information desk, gave my wife's information, and asked to see her. The girl said there was no one in the hospital by that name. I told her, "You must be making a mistake; I was told my wife was here." She asked, "How do you know that?" I said, "Because I'm her husband, I'm the one who called the ambulance, and I was present when she was ushered into the ambulance." She asked for her name and social security number one more time. After giving it to her, she said, "No, she is not here." I requested someone else to speak with; she sarcastically said, "It's not going to make a difference, and how do you know the ambulance brought her to this hospital?" I told her, "Because I spoke to the ambulance dispatcher, and she gave me the ambulance vehicle number along with this hospital's location. That ambulance is sitting outside, so I know my wife is here. I want to see her." The girl told me the same thing; there is no one here by that name.

I could feel myself beginning to lose control. I wanted to grab that smart-ass- chicken-head by her neck and smack the shit out of her. I just turned around and walked outside. I called the hospital patient information number and asked the same questions. I got the same answer. I thought *maybe she was discharged when I fell asleep. Maybe she called me, and I missed her call.* I checked my cell phone, but I had no missed calls. I thought *perhaps she was still upset with me and called her cousin. Maybe she was at home locked out and sitting on the front porch.* I left the hospital, got in the car, and raced home. I called her cousin, but her phone went straight to voicemail. I reluctantly called her daughter for help and explained the situation to her. I asked her if she had heard from her mother.

Calling her daughter was a big mistake and a complete waste of time. Her daughter began to tell me what a shitty husband I was for once again not knowing where my wife was. I was not in the mood to hear her immature bullshit, so I hung up the call. I pulled up into the driveway, hoping to see her there, but she was not. I opened the door and ran inside, calling, "Babe! Babe!" But she was not home. I got back in the car and raced around the corner to see if she was sitting at the park, but she was not there. I went back to the other hospitals and asked if my wife was there, but I got the same answer. I called her phone again, but still, there was no response. I went back home, not knowing what to do.

I accidentally fell asleep again and woke up after 10 am. I called my wife's cell phone, but once again, it went straight to voicemail. I called her cousin, but her phone went straight to voicemail as well. I drove back up to Clovis Community Hospital. I went into the emergency room and up to the check-in desk. There was a different girl at the counter, so I asked again for my wife. I gave my wife's name and social security number, and the girl sarcastically said, "I can't release any information." I said, "But I'm her husband." She told me it did not matter and that my wife's information was to be kept private. I said, "But I'm her husband; I know she was brought here; I'm the one who called the ambulance." She shook her head and said, "It does not matter. It has been requested that none of her information is to be given out to anyone." I asked, "At whose request?" She sarcastically said, "At the patient's request." I was confused, so I asked the girl, "My wife requested that I not see her?"

The girl rolled her eyes, looked at me, smiled, nodded her head, and muttered, "Umm-hmm." (It seemed to give her great pleasure) I fucking lost it! I shouted at her, "How fucking stupid is this hospital! My wife suffered a PTSD flashback and could not answer basic questions to determine whether she should be placed on a 51/50 hold! She was transported to this hospital because obviously, she was not doing well, and you guys listened to her when she asked to have her information blocked?" I shouted, "Was she asked, was she coerced, or was she given a form to sign without knowing what she fucking signed?" Suddenly, the girl sat up straight with a bright red face and acted like she had some common sense. She said, "Sir, all I can tell you is that she was discharged at 8:37 this morning." I repeated, "8:37 this morning?" The girl nodded her head and said, "Yes, sir." I looked at the time; it was almost 11 am. I looked around the emergency waiting room, hoping to see her sitting in a chair asleep; she was not there. I got in the car and raced back home. Around this time, her cousin Mae called me back. I explained to her what had taken place the night before, along with the hospital situation. Mae became worried and said that she had not heard from Crystal, but she would keep trying to reach her by calling her cell phone.

I arrived home, but Crystal was not there. I had no idea where she was. I was exhausted, and I did not know what to do. I could not think. Crystal and I had appointments that Saturday afternoon with our psychologist, Dr. Masters. I logged on to Crystal's telehealth account and waited for the video appointment to start. Dr. Masters came on and said hello. I explained to her what had taken place. Dr. Masters cleared her next meeting and spent the next 2 hours with me online. She contacted every hospital and mental health agency in Fresno, Clovis, Madera, and Visalia, starting with Clovis Community. Everyone she spoke to, had no information as to Crystal's current location or health status. As our video session was about to end, I told Dr. Masters that I would call Fresno P.D and file a missing person report. She said okay, I should keep her informed, and she would still try to help locate my wife.

I got in the car and began to drive around town looking for my wife. I had no real idea what I was doing. I was driving around aimlessly, hoping to spot her somewhere. I got P.D on the phone and spent the next 20-30 minutes filing the missing person report. Due to Crystal's mental illness, I did not have to wait for 24hrs. I filed the report, and they gave me a case number. I came back home and sat at the dining room table. I burst into tears, and I prayed. I prayed like I never prayed before, asking for my wife to be watched over wherever she was and to be returned home to me safely.

It was now after 4 pm on Saturday. I was sitting at the dining room table. I called my wife's brother to ask if he had heard from her. I explained to him what had taken place, and I gave him the case number. Our dining room table faced our kitchen window. Our kitchen window faced down our driveway and out into the street. I was talking to her brother, just staring out of the window, watching cars passing by. I put my head down and began to cry as her brother thanked me for the way I was taking care of his sister. He thanked me for loving her enough to stay with her and help her with her mental illness. I looked up and stared out of the kitchen window as I told him, "Thank you," then something in the window caught my attention.

From where I was sitting, I looked up over the counter but didn't see anything. Her brother was still talking… Then I saw it again. This time I recognized what I had seen, the top of my brown and black beanie! My grandmother had crocheted that beanie for me when I was in high school, and my wife was wearing it that night when we were on our way to the hospital. I stood up and looked out of the window, and it was Crystal trying to run, stumbling up the driveway. I shouted to her brother, it's Crystal! She is running up the driveway!

MANIA/PSYCHOSIS
GOD RETURNED CRYSTAL HOME

C rystal was out of breath, exhausted, and delirious. Her lips were dry, chafed, and bleeding. She had on the same pajamas and jacket that she was wearing the night before; but she was not wearing any shoes, only socks. She fell against the security gate as I cried out, "Babe! What happened?" She was about to pass out, she gasped, "I'm thirsty." I opened the gate, and she fell forward into my arms. I held her up and carried her into the living room to sit her down. She said she needed to use the bathroom, so I carried her to the bathroom and sat her down on the toilet. She was leaning against the wall, trying to hold herself up. I began to cry as I kissed her all over her face, happy and relieved to see her. She reached up and held my face in her hands, trying to kiss me back.

I ran to the kitchen, got her a bottle of water, and ran back to the bathroom. I gave her the water and asked, "Babe, what happened? Where are your shoes?" I kneeled in front of her. I was able to see that Crystal's mental condition had worsened. She had this hysterical look on her face and she could not stop trembling. I looked at her feet, at her socks. They were dirty, dusty, and ripped. I yanked her socks off and checked her feet; they were red, swollen, and bruised. I looked up at her, and she said, "**I left the hospital...I ran home....Something told me...Get up and go home; your husband needs you.**"

I reached up and hugged her, crying, asking, "What do you mean you left the hospital? Why didn't you call me to come to pick you up?" Crystal could not answer my question, she only asked for some more water. I walked down the hall into the kitchen. **I was in a daze as I thought to myself,** *the hospital was 12 miles away. How in the world did she manage to find her way home? Why did they let her go? Why did they allow her to leave in this condition*? I grabbed another water out of the refrigerator and walked back to the bathroom. As I passed the front door, I could see something out of the corner of my eye. I looked, and it was Crystal. She was running full speed down the driveway, towards the street with a pair of boots in her hand. I dropped the water and sprinted out of the front door. I caught up to her, grabbed her coat, and asked, "Babe, where are you going?" She spun around and began to hit me yelling, "Get out of my way! Leave me alone! Help! Help!"

I got her in a bear hug and lifted her off the ground. She began beating me in the face all over again. I said, "Babe, stop!" She was yelling for me to let her go. I would not lose Crystal again, so I purposely began to squeeze her, making it hard for her to breathe. I read some research that suggested if I could safely reduce the oxygen and blood flow to her brain to the point just before she passes out, I might have a chance to calm her down. So, I tightened my hug. She put both of her hands on my shoulders and was trying to push herself away. She said, "I can't breathe." I looked at her and said, "Babe, relax," as I squeezed her some more. Her face was turning red as she struggled for air. I just held onto her. She began to get this dizzy look on her face as she was about to pass out. I lowered her back down onto the ground and lessened my grip while still hugging her. She leaned her head against my chest as she began to catch her breath.

I said, "Babe, I love you. You can't be out here like this; your feet are in bad shape. You just walked home from the hospital." She was still trying to catch her breath as she said, "I don't want to go home." I said, "Ok, where do you want to go?" She said, "For a walk." I told her, "Babe, you can't..." Her personality began to change, she was starting to get upset, so I said, "Ok, ok, ok...at least put your boots on." She calmed down and said, "Ok." She put on her boots and then tried to run again. I grabbed her arm and said, "Hey, hey, we are walking. I will walk with you, but you can't run. It's dangerous; there is traffic all around us". She yanked her arm back and said, "Fine!" She began to speed walk down the sidewalk as I walked beside her.

She began to retrace the path that she used to walk ten years prior when she was upset and left the apartment. I walked alongside her, trying to talk to her; she was walking very fast. Her personality was continually changing from being angry and combative, to being confused and delusional. She was yelling at me, asking, "Why did you call the police on me? All those times you were beating my ass and choking me, I never called the police on you."

I apologized and tried to explain that she was not well and that I was trying to get her to the hospital. She began to cuss me out for calling the cops. I told her, "Babe, I'm sorry for calling 911, but I had no choice. I never requested the police. Every time I called 911, I asked for an ambulance, never the police; the police just showed up." I could tell she was trying to process what I was saying, so I just kept talking as we walked. We walked for miles and miles and for hours. I told her that I loved her and would never do anything to hurt her. I told her that something was going on with her that we need to figure out. I asked if she remembered the pain that was in the back of her head the night before. Crystal looked up and shook her head. She stopped walking for a minute and said that she was getting hot. She was still wearing her P. J's and the oversized coat from Friday. I told her that it was getting dark and cold outside and that she was sweating badly. She could not take off her jacket. I did not want her to catch pneumonia. She became upset and began walking again. She was yelling about how she was tired of me bossing her around. I told her, "I'm sorry it feels like I'm bossing you around, that's not my intention. I'm only trying to take care of you." She stopped walking and told me to stand in front of her. I stood in front of her as she took off her coat and then tried to take off her shirt. I grabbed her shirt and said, "Babe! What are you doing? You can't take your shirt off outside." She yelled, "Let go!" I let her go and stood in front of her. She took off her shirt: bare boobs outside and all. I wrapped the coat around her; she put it on and I zipped it up. She handed me the shirt as we began to walk again. Her bizarre and confusing behavior continued for about 3 hours while we were walking. By this time, she began talking to herself and whoever was in her mind.

It was getting dark, so I told Crystal, "We got to start heading back. We can't be out like this." She was not listening to me. She was just walking and talking to herself like she was in a trance. Then she stopped, looked at me, turned around, and started heading back towards the apartment. She asked for the shirt back so that she could put it on. She asked me not to call the police on her again. I told her I never called the police; I only asked for the paramedics. She yelled at me and asked, "Did I ever call the fucking police on you?" I said, "No babe, you did not." She said, "Then promise me you won't get them on me anymore." I said, "I promise, babe." As we headed back home, we walked along a strip of sidewalk where a fence separated us from the backyards of several houses. She asked me, "Do you have your cell phone?" I said, "Yes, babe." She said, "Let me have it." I asked her, "Why?" She said, "I want to call my brother."

I reached into my back pocket and handed her my cell phone. She took it and ran over to the fence. I asked, "Babe, what are you doing?" as I ran after her. She took the battery out of my phone and threw it over the fence. She said, "Here! Now you can't call the police on me." She turned and began to walk home. I made sure to remember which backyard it was as we walked away. We were almost home when Crystal's legs and feet began to give out on her. She said, "I can't walk anymore. My legs hurt." She leaned up against a tree. I told her to get on my back, and I would carry her the rest of the way home. She refused and said, "No, daddy, I don't want to hurt your back."

I looked at her. Crystal was back. I asked, "Babe?" She said, "Yeah, daddy. I'm here." I knew it was my wife because she hardly ever calls me James, sometimes she calls me babe, but mostly she calls me dad or daddy. She said, "I'm, going to sit right here; I will wait for you. Run home and get the car because I can't walk anymore." I said, "Babe, I just went through hell, not knowing where you were. I'm not going to lose you again." She said, "Daddy, I'm fine. I'm not going anywhere. Just hurry, please, and go get the car." So I took off and sprinted home.

I ran into the condo and grabbed the car keys. I called 911 and requested an ambulance. (I know I promised my wife I wouldn't, but I had to get her back to a hospital) the 911 dispatcher acted like a stupid ass, asking me why I needed an ambulance even though I clearly explained Crystal's current medical condition. I was looking out of the kitchen window, and I saw Crystal running up the driveway again. I hung up the phone and grabbed the keys. I ran to the door and shut it. She yelled, "What were you doing?" I said, "Looking for the car keys." She said, "You were calling the police again, weren't you?" I said, "No, babe. I did not know where the keys were. I took off running after you earlier, remember?" She calmed down and said, "Oh. I want to go and see my cousin." I said, "Ok, let's go."

POPEYES

I locked the front door, and we got into the car. I watched as Crystal put on her seat belt. I drove down the driveway, and I asked, "Babe, how are you feeling?" She said, "I'm ok." I said, "Babe before we go to your cousin's house, I need to go to the home where you threw my battery over the fence." She looked at me and had this scared look on her face. She asked, "Are you mad at me?" She began to pull away. I offered her my hand to hold. I said, "No, babe, I'm not mad at you; I'm happy you are here with me." A look of relief came across her face. She said, "Ok." I drove out of our driveway and around the corner. As I pulled up to the home, she asked, "Are you going to call the police on me when you get your battery?" I said, "No, babe, I'm not. But I need my phone; how else are you going to call me while I'm at work?" She just looked at me. I could see that she was fighting hard to process and accept what I was telling her. I said, "When I get my battery, how about we put it, along with my phone, in the glove box." Crystal breathed a sigh of relief and said, "Ok."

I pulled up to the house. I told her everything would be okay. I also asked her not to leave the car, and if she needed me, she should just shout. She began to panic and asked, "Where are you going to be? Are you leaving?" I said, "No, babe, I'm going to be right there," I pointed to the front door of the home. I told her, "You will be able to see me the entire time." She nodded her head and leaned back in her seat; I shut off the car and got out. I rang the doorbell. A nice white guy came to the door. I told him our child accidentally threw my cell phone battery over his fence into his backyard near his tree. He laughed and said, "That's a new one; what side of the fence was it near, the right or left? I pointed to the right side of his backyard and said, "On the right side, just behind the tree." He said, "Wait right here, let me find my flashlight, and I will take a look." I thanked him. I turned to check on Crystal. She was still sitting in the car staring at me. A few minutes later, the guy came back with my battery. I thanked him and walked away.

I got back into the car and said, "Ok babe, put these in the glovebox please." I gave her my phone and the battery as I promised earlier. She put them in the glove box, looked at me, and said, "Thank you." We drove off. We got to the other side of town and began to look for her cousin's house. It was dark outside. We had only been to her cousin's house once before, a year prior. I could not remember the street or what her neighborhood looked like. Plus, it was during the day when we went. We drove around, and I told Crystal, "Babe, I don't remember which street she lives on. All of the roads look the same." She said, "I know, I can't remember either." I said, "Babe, I have no idea where she lives. Do you want to give her a call? Her number is in my phone." She said, "No, I don't want the phone turned on." I said, "Ok, babe, we can go home, and you can call her from the house phone, get her address, and we can come back." She said, "Ok." So we headed home.

I turned on the radio and put on a smooth jazz station to keep Crystal calm. As we got closer to home, we were approaching a Popeye's chicken. She said, "I'm hungry. Let's eat at Popeye's." I immediately knew Crystal was gone again because she would never eat at Popeye's. She rarely ate fast food, and if she does, it is Chick-Fil-A. I said, "Babe, you don't eat Popeye's, and we don't have money in the bank for fast food. We only have enough for gas." I was coming up to a red light, so I began to slow down. Crystal was starting to get agitated. She shouted, "I want Popeye's!" She realized that I was not in the left turn lane to go to Popeye's, so she took off her seat belt. I grabbed her hand and asked, "What are you doing?" She yelled, "I'm going to Popeye's; I told you I'm hungry!"

I said, "Babe, you can't get out into traffic." She ignored me and opened the door and began to step out of the car. I yelled, "Ok! Fine!" And smashed down on the accelerator pedal. She flew back in her seat as the door slammed shut. I ran the red light, made a U-turn, and headed toward Popeye's. She immediately calmed down as we pulled up to the restaurant and parked. I told her, "Babe, I don't remember how much is in the bank. So you can't get upset if our card gets declined." She said, "It will be ok; let's go get something to eat." I got out and followed her in.

My wife looked a mess like she had been through hell. She was wearing my brown and black beanie with her hair sticking out from underneath it—my baby blue long sleeve thermal, her grey pajama pants with white stars and a pair of black Ugg boots, with one pant leg, tucked in. We walked into the restaurant, and all the people began to stare at us. I put my arm around Crystal and got in line. I asked her what she wanted; she said she was not sure. I let a few people go ahead of us while she decided. She told me that she could not read the menu board, so I moved us to the side, and I read the options to her. She decided on the chicken strips with mashed potatoes and a biscuit. We got back in line and ordered our food. We got our drinks and went to go and sit down. She wanted to sit by the window. We sat our drinks down on the table when Crystal said she needed to use the bathroom. I walked her to the bathroom and waited outside the door. Our order was ready, so I knocked on the bathroom door and told her our food was ready. I got our food and went to our table. I stood there, keeping an eye on the bathroom door to make sure she made it out okay. Crystal came out of the bathroom and went to the counter, asking for our food. I walked over to her; told her I got our food and walked her to our table.

I sat across from her; she was struggling with the battle that was taking place inside her head. One minute she was playful, feeding me French-fries as if we were on our first date. Then she became serious and tried to talk to me about running our finances, like the business owner that she once was. Then she became disconnected, staring out of the window with a blank look on her face. I would have to call her several times before she "came back" to the table. Then she would eat again, being my wife for a brief second, asking me how I was feeling and how work was going. I told her as long as we are together, I am fine. The smile that came across her face was indescribable. She hugged herself and said, "I will always love you." Then she became reticent once again and stared out of the window.

I sat there, trying desperately to be strong as I fought back my tears. I was struggling with the thought that this may be my last meal with my wife. It was painful, watching her struggle to be present. I called her several times again, "Babe, baby, babe, you need to eat before your food gets cold." She slowly turned to look at me. She stared at me for a few seconds with her eyes wide open. It seemed like she was trying to focus on my face, struggling to recognize who I was; I told her I loved her and asked if she was okay. She nodded her head and began to eat. She did not say anything and just ate quietly. After a few minutes, she looked up and asked me if her notepad was still in the back of the car. I told her it was. She asked if I could go outside and get it and bring a pen alongside.

I went outside, grabbed her notepad from the backseat, and grabbed a pen. I came inside and placed them on the table in front of her. She was staring out of the window. I asked, "Babe, are you ok? Did you want to write something down?" It took her a few more seconds before she came back to the table. She looked at me and then wrote, "James, with all my love I need you."

FINALLY, RUSHING CRYSTAL TO THE HOSPITAL

Crystal turned the paper around towards me so I could read what she wrote. She handed me the pen, and I wrote, "I need you too, baby. Please come back to me; please come home to me." Tears rolled down my cheeks as I turned the paper around back towards her so she could read what I wrote. Crystal was able to read it. She looked at me and reached her hand across the table. I held her hand and told her, "I love you." She said, "I love you too."

She began to eat again, struggling, while battling the psychotic thoughts plaguing her mind. I just wanted to spend as much time with her as I could. I did not care about all of the looks, stares, and laughter from people as they walked by. I just wanted to be with my wife regardless of whoever she was at the moment. She looked up and asked if I could order some more mashed potatoes. She said she wanted to eat them at home with the rest of her biscuits. I said, "Ok," and got up. She said she needed to use the bathroom again, so I walked her to the bathroom and went to order her mashed potatoes. I went back and sat at our table, staring at what we wrote on the paper.

I broke down and cried as I stared out of the window, saying to myself, "What am I going to do? How am I going to help my wife?" Something told me to look towards the bathroom. I looked up and saw Crystal talking to one of the female employees. I scooted to the edge of the bench as I saw the employee's eyes get wide with an uncomfortable look on her face. I got up and walked quickly to Crystal—the employee left in a rush behind the counter and out of sight. Crystal was grabbing the back of her head. She looked at me, worried, and said, "I'm sorry."

I asked, "Sorry for what, babe?" She said, "I asked the girl to call the police, the back of my head is hurting, and I want to go to the hospital." I said, "Ok, babe, let's go;" I asked her, "Why did you ask for the police?" She said, "I thought you would be mad at me because I left the hospital earlier today." I said, "No, babe, I'm not angry but let's get out of here before the police come." She said, "Ok." I went to the table and got her notepad. We got in the car and took off, going northbound on Peach Ave; as I sped up the street, three police cars sped past us going southbound with their lights flashing and sirens blaring, probably on their way to the restaurant.

As I approached the freeway, Crystal began to cry, saying that the sharp pain in the back of her head was getting worse. I said, "Ok, babe, I need to get on the freeway to get you to the hospital as fast as I can; you can't open the door and try to get out, ok?" She said, "Ok," but as I approached the freeway on-ramp, she began to panic again. The light was red; I reached over her, reclined her seat back so she could not see outside, and also to try and relieve the pain in the back of her head.

The light turned green. I put my seat belt back on and sped onto the freeway. Crystal was in much pain, crying, begging me to hurry. I grabbed her hand to keep her calm, letting her know that we would be there soon. We arrived at the emergency room, at which I helped my wife out of the car. We walked in and got her checked in. **During the check-in process, I learned that Crystal was placed on a 51/50 hold as a danger to herself earlier that day**. I asked the person checking us in, **"How was my wife able to walk out of the hospital, without seeing a doctor, with that type of diagnosis?"** The person apologized and said they didn't know how that happened.

My wife and I sat in the waiting room for about an hour. A nurse called her name, and we walked into one of the rooms. The nurse asked what brought us to the hospital. I explained my wife's complaint regarding sharp pains at the rear of her skull, above her neck. I explained the PTSD flashbacks and erratic behavior. They said they would get my wife a CT scan and have her talk to the hospital psychiatrist. I waited in the room with Crystal and kept her company, trying to keep her calm. About 1hr later, a nurse came and took her to get the CT scan. I was told to wait in the lobby.

After the scan, they came and got me, and I went back to Crystal's room. She was exhausted, and she fell asleep with her head on my shoulder. She had been awake for about three days. After about another hour, the nurse came to get my wife to see the psychiatrist. I was told to wait in the lobby again. I requested to be present during the visit. They told me it would be up to the psychiatrist. I told Crystal before I walked away, "I will be right outside. If you need me, you ask them to come and get me, ok?" She nodded; I kissed her forehead. She looked scared as I walked away.

I walked to the waiting room, sat, and waited, eventually falling asleep. I woke up later to a hospital staff member standing beside me, calling my name. I woke up, and they asked if I was James, Crystal's husband. I said, "Yes." They asked me to come back to the room; the psychiatrist wanted to speak to me. The staff member said that they had been trying to call my phone for about an hour. I said, "I don't have my cellphone on me." (Still in the glove box with the battery out). I said, "For an hour? Why not just walk out to the lobby and come and get me?" He did not answer me. I walked into my wife's room; she was covered in a blanket. They had her in hospital scrubs, and she was shivering; her room was ice cold. I kissed her and asked if she was ok. She said yes, but she was having trouble talking to the psychiatrist. She was having trouble remembering what had taken place. She was speaking to the psychiatrist via telehealth video. The Dr. introduced himself, and I thanked him for allowing my visit. I began to explain the events that had transpired along with everything that had happened the previous year. He asked me if Crystal had suffered a recent traumatic event. I told him yes. I explained the college incident with the professor and her childhood rape. He apologized for her experiences and said he would prescribe her some medications. He asked if I would be with her or if she had a safe place to stay where someone could watch her. I told him, "Yes, I'm off work for the next two days. He said, "Ok." He thanked me for all of the information and told my wife that she would be discharged soon. I thanked him for his time, and the video screen went blank. I looked at Crystal and asked her how she was doing, and she said, "Drained." I asked her how the pain was in the back of her head. She said her head was sore, but the pain had gone down a little. She said it felt better after she fell asleep on me. We laughed as she apologized for drooling all over my shirt.

EXODUS RECOVERY

T he nurse returned to the room about an hour later and asked me to wait out in the lobby as they prepared my wife to be discharged. I kissed Crystal and told her I would be outside. About 45 minutes later, Crystal came out. I helped her into the car, and as we headed home, she fell asleep. I got off of the freeway and she woke up and looked around in a panic. I grabbed her hand and said, "Hey, babe, it's ok; I'm right here; we are almost home." A sigh of relief came across her face.

I pulled into the driveway, and she asked me to stop the car. I asked, "What's wrong, babe? Tell me what's going on." She said, "I don't know, I can't explain it, all I know is that I can't go into the apartment." I asked, "Why, babe, what are you feeling?" She said, "It feels like Richard is in there." (Richard was her mother's boyfriend that repeatedly beat and raped her as a child. He has been deceased for quite some time.) I said, "Baby, Richard is not in our apartment; he died a long time ago. I am here, and I won't let anything happen to you." Crystal looked at me and kissed me. She grabbed my hand and squeezed it tight and said, "I know, but something is telling me that he is in the apartment waiting for both of us to go in, and when we do, he is going to kill us." I just looked at my wife as I listened to her. She was panicking and genuinely believing what she was telling me. I said, "Ok babe, but you need to get some sleep. Let me go inside and get our pillows and a blanket, and we can sleep out here in the car again. We will go inside tomorrow when it is daytime. How does that sound?" She said, "Ok," and thanked me. She said, "I'm sorry for all of the trouble I'm causing." I told her, **"You don't have to apologize, I love you, and none of this is your fault."**

I drove up to the front of our apartment and parked the car. I opened the door to get out when Crystal grabbed my shirt and began to panic. She yelled, "He is in there! I can see him, please don't go inside! He is going to kill you!" Crystal began to cry. I shut the door, locked us in, and reached over and hugged her. She was shaking badly. I said, "Baby, it is ok. There is no one inside. It's just you and me." She begged me not to go into the apartment. I said, "Ok, babe, let me turn the car on and put on the heater. We will just sleep in here tonight." She said, "Ok," and began to calm down. I wiped the tears from her eyes, turned the heater on, and helped her get comfortable. After a few minutes, we both fell asleep.

Crystal woke up at about 2 am in a panic. I asked her, "What happened babe? How are you feeling? You need to get some sleep." She said, "Take me to Exodus" (A mental health recovery center she was in back in 2013). She said she felt safe there since she had been there before. She said she wanted to go there, get some sleep, and come home after waking up. I told her how proud of her I was and said ok. We left the apartment and headed towards Exodus Recovery.

We arrived at Exodus shortly after 2 am. We walked up to the door and informed security of my wife's request. They checked her in, and I asked to speak to the staff member in charge. "Mandy" came outside and introduced herself. I introduced myself and explained Crystal's current condition. I told her Crystal had not gotten a decent night's sleep in about three weeks. She told me not to worry. They would look up what the hospital prescribed for her, give her the same meds, and allow her to get some rest. She wrote her name and number down on a sticky note and said that I should give her a call if I had any concerns or questions. I gave her our home phone number and my cellphone number. I thanked her and asked to see my wife before I left. She went and got Crystal. She came to the door, and I hugged and kissed her goodbye. I told her to call me in the morning as soon as she woke up. She said, "Ok." She turned and went inside, waving goodbye as the door was closed. I waved as I watched several nurses come to take her information. I went back to the parking lot, got in the car, cried for several minutes, and then left for home. I got home but could not sleep. I was worried about my wife.

I began to clean the apartment. It was a mess; it had not been cleaned in weeks. I called Exodus at around 8 am and asked how Crystal was doing. The staff member that answered told me that she was asleep. I said okay and asked what time were visiting hours. They said that there was no particular time, and I could show up when I wanted. I said I would allow my wife to sleep a few more hours and be there at about 10 am.

I arrived at 10 am to visit. I checked in at the guard station. It took a few minutes before they finally opened the door to let me in, which I thought was odd. I came in, and the guards had me empty my pockets, and patted me down to check for any weapons. Once I was clear, they had me sit and wait for my wife. A few minutes later, a staff member walked over to me. They said Crystal was already in the visitor's room. I thought this was strange because I never saw her walk by. As we walked down the corridor, I asked the staff member, "My wife is already in the visitors' room? How long has she been there?" She did not answer me.

As we got to the room, I walked in, and Crystal was sitting in a chair all alone, rocking back and forth. She was still in her hospital scrubs. She was no longer wearing her beanie, and her hair was a mess. She turned to look at me and held out her arms. She opened and closed the palms of her hands like a baby when it wants an adult to pick them up. She looked hysterical and delusional. She was shaking and drooling on her shirt. She tried hard to focus her eyes on me as she swayed, sitting in the chair. She was trying hard to speak like she was trying to tell me something but only babbling like her brain had been fried.

I sat down next to her, held her face as I looked at her, and said, "Babe, what happened? What did they do to you?" She began to kiss me all over my face, frantically. Crystal was trying so hard to explain to me what had taken place, but she could not. She was only able to mutter a few words, babbling, and drooling. I held her and cried. I became FUCKING FURIOUS! I told her, "Hold on, babe, I will be right back." I got up and walked to the nurse's station and shouted, "WHAT THE FUCK DID YOU GUYS DO TO MY WIFE!" I wiped the tears from my eyes. The security guards began to approach me. I pointed at them and yelled, "DON'T EVEN TRY IT!" I turned back towards the nurse's station and shouted, "That woman in there is not my wife! That's not the woman I dropped off here earlier this morning! WHAT HAPPENED? WHAT DID YOU DO TO HER?"

A staff member walked over to me and asked me to calm down. I told her to get "Mandy;" I wanted to speak to the girl that checked in my wife. I turned and walked back to the visitors' room. I took Crystal's face and held it once again. I said, "Baby. Baby, please, if you can, look at me". She was trying hard to keep her head still. It was like she was a zombie but childlike. I told her, "Babe, look at me; look at me. Try to focus, try to tell me what they did to you."

Crystal was trying hard to speak. She began to flail her arms around like there had been some type of struggle. She grabbed her arm and put it behind her back and mumbled, "Grabbed me." I asked, "Someone grabbed you?" She said, "UmmHmm." Whatever took place disturbed her because she began to panic. At that time, a staff member walked in. My back was towards the door, so Crystal saw them enter the room first. She leaned back in her chair with fright, shaking her head negatively. I turned and looked as I stood up; it was a white woman. She looked to be in her mid- 30's. She introduced herself as the head nurse in charge. I told her, "I asked to speak to Mandy. She apologized and said, "Mandy worked the previous shift and has gone home. That whole shift has gone home. Is there something that I can help you with?"

I told her, "I want to know what happened to my wife. This was not the condition I left her in when we came here earlier this morning." The nurse asked, "What do you mean?" I said, "I brought my wife here a little after 2 am. She came as a voluntary walk-in. All she wanted to do was get a good night's sleep. She was afraid to go into our apartment..." I caught myself explaining to this woman; I stopped and said, "Wait, I explained all of this to Mandy. This info should be documented in my wife's file. Have you read my wife's file yet?" The woman apologized and said that she had not. She explained she just arrived due to the shift change. She said she would go and review my wife's file and be right back. She turned and left.

I sat back down and began to console my wife. Crystal once again began trying to explain what had taken place. I told her to stay calm and just relax, that I would get to the bottom of what took place. I held her and put her head on my shoulder. I began to rock her back and forth, humming our lullaby to keep her calm. A few minutes later, the nurse walked in with my wife's chart. We both looked up from our seats as she began to explain.

"It looks like shortly after you left, your wife was asking to go home," she was reading notes from Crystal's chart. "Your wife became upset when they would not let her leave. They gave her some medication to take, but your wife spat it out and became aggressive. They had to grab her and subdue her...." I stopped her and asked, "Why did they refuse to let my wife leave if she came here voluntarily?" The nurse said, "They placed her on a 51/50 hold, which comes with a Mandatory 48-72 hr. stay." I asked, "51/50, based on what? Who made that determination?" The nurse looked back through my wife's chart and said, "I don't see who made that decision." I asked her, "So what did they give her once she was "subdued"? The nurse said, "It's a standard protocol to provide an injection of 50mg of Trazodone, 50mg of Benadryl, and 2mg of Ativan to patients that display hostile behavior." "Hostile behavior? What type of hostility did my wife show for this to take place?" I asked.

The nurse thumbed through some more pages and said, "It says, here your wife began to bang her head against the concrete walls and floors." I repeated, "Bang her head against the walls and floors? Was this before, after, or during the injection?" The nurse thumbed through some more pages and said, "I'm sorry it does not specify?" I told her, "I want to review the video recording of this incident." She asked, "Recording?" I said, "Yes; from the surveillance cameras you have in this place, you have them everywhere. I want to review what happened." Her face got red, and she seemed uncomfortable. She said, "We don't record anything; we use the cameras to monitor the patients."

I felt like she was bull-shitting me, but I tried to calm down. I did not want them to take their frustrations with me out on Crystal after I left. So I said, "I would like to take my wife home right now." The nurse apologized and said that I could not take her home. Her minimum stay would be 48 hours due to the 51/50 hold. I just shook my head. The nurse said that my wife was due to be seen by a psychiatrist. I told the nurse I wanted to be present during my wife's visit with the psychiatrist. The nurse said, "It won't be for a couple of hours, and it will be a video conference, not an in-person visit." I said, "That's ok; I will wait." The nurse said, "I'm not sure if you could be present during the visit; I have never seen such a thing done before at this facility." I told her, "Of course, I can be present. I'm her husband, and besides, she is in no good condition to talk to any doctor independently. I want to make sure the doctor gets all of the information they need to make an informed decision regarding my wife." The nurse looked at me and said, "Your wife needs to sign a Hippa waiver." I told her, "That's fine. Go and get the paperwork, please."

The nurse walked away angrily. I turned to Crystal and tried to get her attention, saying, "Baby look at me. Look at me. I need you to stay calm ok." She nodded her head and mumbled, "Mean to me." I said, "I know, baby. That is why I need you to be calm; we can't give them a reason to treat you bad, ok." Crystal nodded her head. I told her, "The nurse is coming back with some paperwork. I need you to sign it for me, and I'm going to be with you when you talk to the doctor." Crystal looked at me with a little smile and nodded. The nurse returned and handed my wife the paper. I took it from Crystal and read over the form. I wrote the date and put the pen in Crystal's hand. I said, "Okay baby, I need you to sign right here." She took the pen and scribbled on the paper; I signed below her mark and handed the form to the nurse. The nurse told me that her appointment would not be for a couple of hours. I asked her what time was the meeting scheduled. She said, "Around 2 pm." I told her that I would be waiting outside in the parking lot and would come in at 1:30 pm. I gave her my cell phone number and asked her to call me if Crystal's appointment would start sooner or when the doctor was ready to see my wife. She said, "Ok." She apologized for the way my wife had been treated. I told her to thank you as I helped Crystal to her feet. I held her as we walked towards the exit. I told Crystal I would be back soon and to take her medication when they gave it to her. She nodded her head. I gave her a hug and a kiss and walked out. I went and sat in the car and cried my heart out as I punched the steering wheel and repeatedly banged my fist against the passenger seat and dashboard. I was exhausted. Eventually, I fell asleep.

The nurse called me a couple of hours later to let me know that Crystal was next to see the doctor. I got out of the car, walked across the parking lot, and came inside. The guards checked me in; I sat down and waited for the visit. The nurse came and got me, and I followed her into a room with a big flat screen T.V mounted on the wall. Crystal was sitting in a chair in front of the T.V. She was asleep. Another woman was sitting in the room; she did not introduce herself. She just sat there staring at me as I walked in.

I asked the nurse, "who is the strange woman in the corner?" The nurse told me it was protocol to have a staff member present during the doctor's visit. I said, "That's fine, but I asked you, who is she? What is her title?" The nurse did not respond. She seemed uncomfortable with my questions. I just sat down next to my wife as I stared back at the strange woman. I took Crystal's hand and said, "Baby, baby, I'm here." She woke up and turned toward me. It took her a minute to shake off the grogginess as she tried to focus on my face. When she realized it was me, she smiled and leaned her forehead against my cheek. She had a paper towel in her hand. I took it and wiped the drool from the corners of her mouth and chin. The T.V screen came on, and there was a young white man on the video. He introduced himself He was the psychiatrist.

I introduced both myself and my wife. The psychiatrist went through my wife's paperwork and asked my wife to introduce herself on her own. She did as she fought to stay awake. I told the doctor that I would be speaking on my wife's behalf due to the condition that she was currently in. He asked why she was so groggy; I told him what had taken place as he looked through her chart. He read what they had injected her with and agreed it was too much of a dose. Crystal mumbled to the doctor, "I feel like I have been hit by a truck, and it is hard for me to stay awake." He apologized and told her the medication should wear off in about a day. He asked how she was feeling. Crystal said, "A little better since I was able to get a little rest." The doctor asked me what brought my wife to the facility. So, I began to narrate and explain the entire story.

Her visit lasted for about 45 minutes. The doctor said that my wife might be transferred to a behavioral health hospital for further diagnosis. I said, "If that is the case, can she be transferred to

Community Behavioral Health?" He looked through her chart. He asked if she had been there before. I told him, "Yes, back in 2013-2014." I told him I felt it would be the right place for her to be because she was familiar with the facility. He thanked me for the information, wrote down my request, and thanked me for being present. I thanked him too for his time, and the video ended. The strange woman sitting in the corner got up and walked out of the room. The primary nurse returned and asked me if I wanted to stay and visit with my wife for a few more minutes. I said, "Yes, thank you."

Crystal and I walked back to the visiting room. I stayed with her for about thirty minutes. The injection of medication they gave her had worn off a little bit. She was able to speak a bit more without drooling as much. She said she wanted to come home, having missed me much. I told her that I missed her also as tears ran down my face. She wiped my tears and apologized for everything that was happening. I looked at her and told her, "Do not be sorry." **I reminded her that she had done nothing wrong, none of this was her fault, and that we would make sure she got better.** She just put her forehead against mine and began to cry. I cried as I held her for the remainder of the visit.

The next day was Monday. I called Exodus at 6 am and asked if my wife was coming home or whether she was going to be transferred to a hospital. They told me that she would be transferred to a hospital, but they were unsure which one. I thanked them and hung up. I called the intake department at Community Behavioral Health Hospital and spoke to the nurse. I asked if they had any beds available; she told me they were full at the moment, but they had some patients due to be discharged later that morning. I explained to her that my wife was at Exodus recovery. I explained that Crystal had been a patient at Community Behavioral in the past and hoped to get transferred there that morning. The nurse informed me that my wife's name had been placed on their waiting list and was waiting for a bed to become available. I thanked her for her time and the information and hung up. I called Exodus back and asked them if there was anything that I could do to make my wife's transition to her hospital of choice happen. They informed me the Hospital had been in contact with them. My wife was next to be transferred to Community Behavioral; I thanked them and asked if I could be present during the transfer process. They said yes and that she was scheduled to leave their facility at 10 am. I thanked her and hung up. I left for work. I had to be there at 7 am.

I arrived at work, talked to our foreman and let him know that my wife was not doing well and was due to be transferred to a hospital at 10 am. I asked him if it was okay to leave work to be there during the transfer. He said, "No problem." I worked until 9:30 am, and then went to Exodus. When I arrived, the ambulance was already there. As soon as I checked in with security, a staff member came and got me and said that my wife was distraught and refusing to leave. She told me Crystal said, "She did not want to go to another hospital and wanted to go home." I asked her, "Where is my wife now?" The girl said, "She is still in her room." I asked her, "Can you tell my wife that I am here?" She said yes and left.

Crystal came out of her room, walked down the hall, and came into the visitors' room. She was upset. I asked her to tell me what was wrong. She began to cry and said that she was tired of all the hospital visits and just wanted to come home. I told her that she had to go to one more hospital to get some help. She argued that she was feeling fine and did not want to go to another hospital. I told her that it was out of our hands at this point. She became agitated with me, demanding that I take her home. She said, "That's bullshit; you are my husband. You have the right to get me out of here and take me home!" I told her, "I can't babe; you have been placed on a 51/50 hold and are being transferred to the hospital.

I tried to hug her, but she pushed me away, telling me that I was wrong and never wanted to see me again. I said, "What babe?" She said, "You heard me; just get out of here and don't come back." The nurses just looked at me. I said, "Babe, me leaving here is not going to help you. You don't have a choice; you are being taken to the hospital. Please don't get angry and resist. I don't think your mind and body will be able to handle another dose of whatever they choose to inject you with. That shit is not good for you. I left work so I could be here to make sure everything went okay during your transfer."

"I'm going to follow you in the ambulance to the other hospital. I'm going to be here every step of the way." Crystal folded her arms and looked down at the ground. I asked the nurse, "Is there anything I need to sign?" The nurse said, "Yes." She left and returned with the transfer form. I told Crystal, "Here babe, you have to sign this." She refused to sign it; so I signed for her. I put my arm around her as we walked, but she pushed my arm off her shoulder. She walked to the paramedics with her arms folded and her head down.

I walked alongside her telling her how hard I knew the whole thing was on her, and I'm proud of her for being so strong. She walked over to the gurney and sat down. The paramedics strapped her in and put her into the ambulance. Crystal was staring at me as tears rolled down her face. I felt helpless and sad. I told her everything was going to be alright and that she would be able to look out of the rear window of the ambulance and see me in the car right behind her. I also told her that I would meet her at the other hospital. She leaned her head back onto the pillow and looked away. I thanked the paramedics for their time, and they said, "No problem." They told me that they would be taking freeway 41. I said, "Ok, I will be right behind you."

We arrived at the hospital about 30 minutes later. I parked and got out as the ambulance was unloading Crystal. I waved hi and smiled, but she was still sad. I told her I would be there during visiting hours, and I told her not to forget to put me down on her visiting list. Crystal began to cry as they rolled her inside. I left and returned to work.

The remainder of my day at work was difficult. I spent most of the time in the bathroom, crying. I called the hospital on my lunch break to see how my wife was doing. They told me she had gone through the intake process and was being taken to her room. I asked if Crystal put my name down as her emergency contact on her visitors list. They said, "Yes, you are on all her paperwork. We transferred her information from her chart at Exodus Recovery." I thanked them and hung up. I later went back to work when my lunch break was over.

I arrived at the hospital at 6:10 pm. Visiting time did not start until 6:30 pm, but the security staff had to check me in and go through the bag of clothes that I brought for Crystal. I packed a bag while I was at home. Two bars of dove unscented soap (one for her face and one for her body), her toothbrush, five pairs of socks and panties, three pairs of pajamas, one pair of slippers, one pair of boots, two pairs of jeans, and two shirts. After check-in, I was given my name tag and I walked to her unit. I rang the doorbell, and the staff buzzed me in. I gave them her bag of belongings so that they could make an inventory of all of her stuff.

I went into the visiting room as they went to go and get Crystal. A few minutes later, she came walking in and was happy to see me. She was still struggling to be calm, but she was pleased to see me. I gave her a big hug and many kisses. I asked how she was feeling. She said, "I'm tired and just want to come home." I said, "I know, babe. I want you to come home too, but we got to get you the help that you need." She said, "I know, I just want this to be over; I'm tired of the hospitals." I looked at her and said, "Well…if you stop running all over town like you are Forest Gump, you would not be here." Crystal laughed when I said this. It felt good to hear Crystal laugh again. We spent the rest of the visit holding hands and talking.

Crystal spent about six days in the hospital before she was able to come home. The doctor prescribed her Trintellix, Clonazepam, and Olanzapine. The medication seemed to work while she was at the hospital, but after about a week of being at home, her psychosis became worse. Eventually, she had to go back to the hospital and stay for about another six days. When she returned home, she suffered yet another incident—this time, with "Self-harm."

THE VOICES-SELF HARM

◆•————————•————————•◆

C rystal was in the bathroom in front of the mirror. I was sitting down on the toilet. I was not using the bathroom; I was sitting on top of the seat, keeping her company. She was doing okay. Not well, but better than the norm. I was already dressed; we were getting ready to go to the grocery store. I was just waiting for her to finish curling the ends of her hair. Crystal's hair was braided into these long braids, and she was going back and forth doing her makeup and fixing her hair. She said, "I am almost finished getting ready; you might want to warm up the car." I said, "Ok, babe, I will be right back." I left the bathroom, went to our bedroom, put on my shoes, and then proceeded to walk to the front door, passing back by the bathroom. Our bathroom had a massive mirror on the wall. It went from the counter, where the sinks were, up to the ceiling. Something told me to look in. I could see Crystal in the reflection of the mirror. She had this wild, hysterical look in her eyes, and she had the scissors. She was frantically pulling and cutting out her braids, down to her scalp in some sections.

I rushed in and shouted, "Babe!" I grabbed her wrist and pulled her hand away from her head. I tried to remove the scissors from her hand, but she curled her fingers around the finger loops and would not let go. She was yelling and hitting me, telling me to leave her alone. I was shouting, "Babe, give me the scissors!" I lost my composure for a second and panicked in the process. I quickly returned to my senses and realized how dangerous this situation had become; we were both tussling around the bathroom with a pair of sharp hair salon scissors in my wife's hand.

I had her behind me, with her arm trapped in front of me, extended outward. Her fingers were still locked into the loopholes of the scissors. I asked her as calmly as I could, "Babe, why are you cutting your hair." She yelled, "Because I don't need it anymore! I'm going to cut my hair and then go for a walk!" She tried to break free from my grip, hammer fisting me on my back and the back of my head. I asked again, "Babe, what do you mean?" She yelled, "I just don't need it anymore; now let me go!" I said, "Ok. You don't need your hair anymore; at least let me cut and style your hair for you. Remember how I cut your hair short years ago?" She calmed down a little and said, "No, thank you, I can do it myself." I said, "Ok. I'm going to let you go so you can finish cutting your hair. Are you sure you can do it?" She said, "Yes, you can watch me if you want to." I said, "Ok, but if you need my help, I'm going to be right here, ok." She said, "Okay." I could feel her body and arm relax.

I looked at her reflection in the mirror, and her face was relaxed. I slowly let her go as I watched her. She had this fake smile on her face, trying to indicate to me that she was okay. She began to cut out long braid after long braid. I stood there, helpless. I could feel the tears rolling down my cheeks as I watched her go from slowly cutting off her hair to working herself back up into the frenzy that she was in before I walked into the bathroom. I could not take it anymore; the level of despair took over me as I watched Crystal. She began jabbing herself on her head with the scissors, yanking and pulling hard on her hair, bending her neck in the process. I burst into tears and rushed to my wife, grabbing her arm away from her head and pinning her against the wall. I began sobbing, asking her, "Baby, what are you doing? You're not okay, babe. We have to take you back to the hospital." I think my actions startled my wife back into reality because she got really quiet and then leaned her whole body against me and began to cry. It was as if she was saying, "I give up."

I took the scissors from her hand and put them into my back pocket. I sat her down on the toilet and kneeled in front of her. I said, "Baby... I love you very, very much. You are my life, but you are not doing well right now. We have to take you back to the hospital." She nodded her head. I told her, "Before we go, you have to let me fix your hair. You have cut off a lot of it." She nodded her head in affirmation. I took the scissors from my back pocket and cried as I cut off the remainder of my wife's long braids. She stopped me after a while and said, "Just take me. I'm ready to go." I said, "Baby, I'm not done with your hair." She said, "It does not matter; just call the ambulance so they can take me." I said," Ok, c'mon, let's call them together." I picked her up and held her as we walked into the dining room. We sat down at the table, and I got the police non-emergency line and asked the dispatcher for an ambulance. The paramedics arrived about 5 minutes later.

When the paramedics arrived, they said hello and asked what the emergency was. I told them my wife was not feeling well and needed to be taken back to Community Behavioral Health Hospital. They apologized and said they could not transport my wife to the hospital directly. She would need to be admitted into Exodus Recovery and transferred over or go in as a voluntary walk-in. I did not know this, so I thanked them and apologized for the call. I informed them I would take my wife myself. They said, "Ok, but if things take a turn for the worse, don't hesitate to call us back." I thanked them and shut the door. I looked at Crystal and said, "C'mon babe, I need to take you." I went to get a beanie to cover her head, but she refused to wear it and said, "I don't want it. Just take me."

We got into the car and headed to the hospital. This time I did not get on the freeway. I drove surface streets. The hospital was about 12 miles away. I was trying to spend as much time with her as possible before I dropped her off. I held her hand the entire way. She was very quiet. She was just staring out of the passenger window with a look of defeat on her face. We arrived at the hospital, and as I pulled into the handicapped parking stall, she whispered to me inaudibly, "Just let me go."

I asked, "Babe, did you say something?" She said, "Yes…just let me go." I parked the car, shut it off, and asked, "What do you mean?"

She turned and looked at me with tears in her eyes and said, "Daddy, you don't deserve to go through what I'm putting you through. You don't deserve a life like this. You are still young enough to start over with someone else. Start a new life; start your own family. You don't deserve to be unhappy anymore. All I do is make you sad. So when you drop me off, don't come back. I will be ok."

I tried to be strong, but I could not stop the tears from running down my face. I took and held the back of Crystal's hand against my forehead. It's my gesture of "Bowing" to her like the queen she is. I started that tradition many, many years ago. It's my way of saying, "I love you and there is no place else I would rather be" in one gesture of affection. I cried as I told her, "You are my love; you are my life, you are my wife. You are the air that I breathe. You are the sun on my face. You are the first person I think about when I wake up. I miss you when you are gone, and I miss you when you are sitting right next to me. I will never let go of you. We WILL figure this out. We WILL get you better."

Crystal cried as I spoke to her. When I was done, I kissed her forehead, and we got out of the car. Covid-19 had just struck, so then the hospital made us wait outside. They brought my wife the paperwork to fill out, but they said they were currently full and did not have any beds available. They said we could return later that evening and try again. We got back into the car and returned home. When we got inside, I asked her, "How do you feel?" She said she was not sure. I said, "Ok babe, well, I need to do something about your hair. I can't let you walk around like that." She said, "Ok." We went into the bathroom, and I got my clippers and styled her hair. For the remaining moments of that evening, she was very calm.

CRYSTAL'S CONDITIONS, PUTTING THE PUZZLE TOGETHER

C rystal had been suffering from these hallucinations off and on for years, close to a decade. We just did not know at the time what it was, but everything was beginning to make sense. I thought back to the previous years when she was smoking marijuana to alleviate her pain from Paget's disease. The CBD in the cannabis helped relieve her pain; however, the THC in the cannabis caused her hallucinations to become more intense, making her thoughts progressively worse. Now she was on these medications, but they seemed to intensify her condition. I went online and thoroughly began to research the medication that she was on. I watched countless video testimonies of people that had been taking many of these medications. I watched numerous videos of different doctors, psychiatrists, and nurse practitioners explaining these meds. I read article after article about these medications. I began to study the warning signs and changes in behavior and thoughts of people with bipolar disorder, schizophrenia, depression, PTSD, anxiety, etc....etc. I went online to different forums and read stories of people struggling with these types of illnesses. Then I began to read about how to help my wife with her feelings and symptoms. I already had become familiar with her PTSD, depression, Bipolar, and anxiety disorders, but the hallucinations were a whole new learning experience for me. I learned that there were several types of hallucinations that Crystal was battling; Auditory, visual, tactile, and olfactory.

I was familiar with the first two hallucinations- auditory and visual hallucinations. The auditory hallucinations meant she was hearing voices that were not there. The visual hallucinations meant she was seeing things that were not there. Tactile hallucinations have to deal with the sense of feeling and or touch. Crystal was feeling things that were not touching her. Olfactory hallucinations meant she was smelling things that were not present.

The visual hallucinations: Crystal began to talk, argue, and cuss at people that were not in our apartment. And when I say cuss and argue, I mean full-on yelling, shouting, and screaming at people she was seeing which I didn't see. She would wake up in the middle of the night, jump out of bed and yell out someone's name and tell them to get the fuck out of our apartment. She would open the front door and cuss out whomever she was seeing, shouting, "Get the fuck out of here, you are not welcome here." She would open the bathroom window and cuss out whomever she "Saw" or open the back porch sliding window and chase out whomever she "Saw" in our apartment. There were also times when she would fix an "Extra" plate of food when we sat down to eat dinner. She would leave the plate on the counter and tell whoever she saw that dinner was ready.

Along with the visual hallucinations were the auditory hallucinations. She kept hearing these voices. It was different from her yelling at or talking to people that were not there. Those people never talked back or spoke to her; it was just visual. The auditory hallucinations she was suffering from were brutal. She was hearing these voices that were continually tormenting her, telling her things like they were going to kill her; they were going to kill me, they were going to kill her children, and try to convince her that she was going to hell. **They were telling her to run out into traffic and get hit by a car. (Code words "Go for a walk")** They would beg her to kill me. They would tell her to take one of the knives that she hid and slit my throat or cut off my penis while I slept. They would beg her to stab me in my sleep. They would call her a dirty nigger, call her a bitch and a slut. They said they would kill her for reporting the professor who sexually harassed her...like I said, brutal. At one point in time, the voices told her that while she was in the hospital, the FBI placed a probe into her brain that allowed them to see what she was thinking and hear what she was saying. They knew her every move. This would keep her in a constant state of panic. I went as far as to purchase an EMF scanner. I would have to stand my wife in front of the bathroom mirror, naked, and "Wand" her down to show her nothing was planted into her body or head. I prayed every time I turned on the scanner that it would not pick up a random frequency signal and cause the alarm to sound. Sometimes, this scanning process was enough to calm her down.

During Crystal's struggle with the auditory hallucinations, she later confessed to me she had been trying to talk to them, reason with them, asking them why they were picking on her and why they would not leave her alone. I asked her, "Babe, how long have you been doing that?" "For a long time," she answered. It pained my heart to hear her say this. **I began to reflect, and I realized all of the times**

I would see her "Talking to herself," she was not; she was talking to these voices. I asked her, "How come you never told me?" She said, "I did not want to worry you, and I did not want to be locked away in a mental institution."

The tactile hallucinations dealt with Crystal's sensation of touch or a feeling. She often felt something crawling around under her skin, and also felt like her heart and stomach had been removed from her body. She would frequently lift her shirt in a panic to show me the "Snake" slithering around in her back. She would run to me crying and begging me to get a knife and cut it out of her. She would also make me lie down with my head on her chest to see if I could check for a heartbeat to make sure her heart was still in her body. On countless nights I would lay down on top of my wife, with my ear over her chest until she fell asleep.

The olfactory hallucinations dealt with Crystal's sense of smell. She was smelling things that were not happening. She often talked about smelling something burning or a strong odor of feces.

I watched my wife struggle with all these hallucinations and disorders for years, with no understanding of what was actually happening. All I could do was hug her, hold her or leave her alone while she was being tormented.

There was one evening when Crystal and I were sitting at the dining room table. I was reading her a story when I looked up and realized that something was on her mind. I asked her what she was feeling, and she told me the voices were talking to her. I asked her, "Is it a man or a woman's voice? She said, "It's a man." I asked her, "How long has he been talking to you?" "The whole time you have been reading," she replied. "Can you tell me what he is saying?" She closed her eyes for a few seconds and said, "He told me to tell you that you are fucking irritating, and he wishes you would shut the fuck up."

I was shocked. I was speechless for a second. I looked at Crystal as her eyes started to fill with tears. I reached across the table, held her hand, and asked, "Do they always talk to you like that?" She said, "He does; he is very mean to me." I asked, "Do you know who he is? Do you recognize his voice?"

"He said to shut the fuck up and mind your own fucking business," Crystal replied. "Who said that?" I asked. "He did," Crystal answered. I told her, "You tell him for me, I said, to go and fuck himself and to leave you alone." She closed her eyes again for a few seconds. She opened them and said, "He is going to kick your ass."

I looked at Crystal's forehead and said, "Ok, Mr. Tough guy, you know where I live. I will be waiting for you at the front door!" "He just called you a dumb nigger." I got up on Crystal's forehead and shouted, "Look here, you little dick "mutha-fucka," if you don't stop fucking with my wife, I'm going to shove my fingers up her nose and smack the shit out of you!" Crystal opened her eyes after a few seconds, looked up, and darted her eyes around. She smiled and said, "He's gone… he left…thank you, babe, because I'm not as good with the insults like you." I said, "Shit, the way you have been chewing on my ass for the last couple of years, you could have fooled me." We both laughed. That punk-ass dude did not bother my wife for the next couple of days.

One afternoon, earlier that year in January, Crystal bought these hunting knives, the kind you take when you go camping. They were brand new. She found them at a thrift store. She bought seven of them. She brought them home and stashed them around the apartment, hiding them in different areas. I caught her one day and I asked her what she was doing, and she said, "I'm hiding these all over the apartment just in case someone breaks in here; I will be able to protect you." I would ask her repeatedly, "Babe, protect me from what and who?" But she would not answer me; **I knew then that she was trying to protect us from the guy that I was arguing with in her head. This was also the same guy that made her cut off her hair and had been telling her to jump out of the car while I was driving or go and run into traffic and commit suicide. Code word "GO FOR A WALK."**

These hallucinations became worse during the evenings and early morning hours. I spoke to the prescribing doctor about Crystal's symptoms and how they seemed to worsen upon taking the medications. The doctor said she would have to continue to take the medications for a couple of months. "The medication needs time to build up in her bloodstream before seeing any real benefits," the doctor would say. Although I understood this concept, I could tell my concerns were kind of going in one ear and out of the other. I thanked him for his time and hung up. Something just did not seem right. I would have to figure this out on my own.

THE "GHETTO HOOD SCIENTIST," SAVING MY WIFE

◆•————————•————————•◆

Disclaimer: "I am in no way, shape, or form a doctor or therapist of any type. I never went to medical school, and I never went to a pharmacological college. I am just a husband that did everything within my power to care for my wife's mental health disorder. I am going to share what I did to help my wife. Please consult your own doctor or health care practitioner for advice."

I will try and keep it simple and explain what I did so that it does not involve all of the medical jargon I had to learn and decipher. I filed for family leave from work for six weeks so that I would be able to thoroughly monitor my wife 24hrs a day, 7 days a week. I will explain what took place from February 2020 through March and into late April of 2020.

As I stated earlier, I began to research my wife's medication. I also began to examine CBD oil and its experimental treatment for schizophrenia and other mental health disorders.

I found that most of the anti-depressants, SSRI's (Selective Serotonin Reuptake Inhibitors), and anti-psychotic medications Crystal was taking came with horrible side effects. They were making her current symptoms worse; for example, she was not sleeping for days at a time, and her anxiety was through the roof. The medication Trintellix was supposed to help with her serotonin levels (A happy mood chemical in the brain); however, it was making her insomnia and anxiety worse. Zoloft was also doing the same thing. Also, due to her insomnia, she was prescribed Ambien but her inability to sleep worsened. (Yes, a possible side effect of Ambien is insomnia). So, she was not sleeping and became more agitated and aggressive than usual.

I found that doctors will often prescribe "Off-label" medication, which means they will prescribe a particular medication for treating a symptom that you don't have, with the hopes that it will treat a symptom you do have. For example, my wife was prescribed Clonazepam, 0.5mg, three times a day. It is a medication used to treat people that suffer from seizures. My wife was not epileptic nor was ever suffering from any seizures; however, this medication's "Side effect" has been shown to help people suffering from depression or panic disorders. In my wife's case, this was not the situation. This medication made her depression and mania worse. Crystal began having more severe thoughts of suicide, and the drug made her auditory hallucinations worse, thus becoming "Command hallucinations." The name says it all. The voices were now commanding her to do certain things, and she was now following their instructions. Thus, grabbing the scissors and cutting off all her hair, and trying much harder to go outside and commit suicide by running into oncoming traffic.

Perhaps, one of the most disturbing Hallucinations my wife suffered from, was the voices of little children. Crystal would hear the voices of children crying and begging her to take them to the park. Crystal was often late picking me up from work because she would drive to one of our local parks and spend hours there day after day, to make the "Kids happy."

I discovered that due to Crystal's mental status, one 0.5mg dose of Clonazepam was like taking a shot of whiskey, and the doctor prescribed she take it three times a day.

Once again, I asked the doctor to take her off these medications. He refused, insisting that she remain on them until they built up in her bloodstream. I decided to take her off myself…cutting her pills in half, slowly tapering her off (Dosing down). I used CBD oil, cracked cell wall Chlorella, Griffonia seed, and other supplements during this process. I also stopped her from eating any fast food and processed foods. If it came in a bag, can or box, we didn't eat it. I bought a new juicer and began juicing organic green vegetables.

Griffonia is a type of plant found in West Africa. Its seeds have a chemical in them called 5-hydroxytryptophan, otherwise known as 5-HTP. This supplement is believed to help raise serotonin levels in the brain. This supplement is important because serotonin helps regulate mood and behavior. Also, I found it to have a positive effect on my wife's mood and level of anxiety and insomnia. I purchased a powder form of it on Amazon. I gave her the lowest recommended serving daily while tapering her off Trintellix. I did this for a month. I also gave her a cracked cell wall Chlorella.

Chlorella is an algae full of vitamins and minerals. It contains Vitamin B12, Vitamin C, and Iron as well as small amounts of magnesium, zinc, copper, potassium, calcium, and folic acid. Chlorella is also a complete source of protein. It contains all 9 essential amino acids. Chlorella is believed to have the ability to remove toxins and impurities from your body. I gave her one teaspoon twice a day in 24 ounces of water in the hopes it would quickly remove the Clonazepam from her system. I also purchased four bottles of THC free CBD oil.

I bought one bottle of CBD oil which was 2500mg (83mg per dropper), and three bottles of CBD oil which were 1000mg (33mg per dropper). I started with 33mg twice a day for four days (66mg). Then 83mg once a day for four days. Then 83mg twice a day for four days (166mg). Then 83mg twice a day, along with 33mg once a day (199mg). I used CBD oil to combat potential adverse withdrawal symptoms/side effects of tapering her off of these medications. My research indicated that 200mg of CBD oil daily was a "Therapeutic starting dose." I was trying to get my wife to this level as quickly and safely as possible.

I also began to re-introduce and increase the number of specific B Vitamins in my wife's body. I started with Niacin (B3). It is believed that people who suffer from a Niacin deficiency may have symptoms of depression, anxiety, and sometimes memory loss. Niacin also helps the body metabolize an amino acid called tryptophan for Serotonin production, Serotonin is one of the two neuro-transmitting chemicals in the brain that regulate mood. The other chemical is Dopamine. I began to give my wife 500mg of Niacin twice a day, in the "No-flush" form (Inositol Hexanicotinate). I gave her the no-flush niacin so she would not experience the harsh, itchy, tingling sensation in the skin that comes from taking regular forms of niacin (Nicotinic Acid). This sensation is referred to as "Niacin flush." This flush is harmless, but it can be very uncomfortable, and since my wife was suffering from Tactile Hallucinations, I did not want to aggravate her symptoms of touch or feel unnecessary. After a couple of weeks, I later went down in dosage to 500mg daily, then down to 300mg daily. After her tactile hallucinations were gone, I began to give her the regular form of Niacin, Nicotinic Acid. I started with 100 mg twice a day with meals. I did this for 8 days. Then I moved her up to 300mg a day for a week, then to 400mg, and finally to 500mg a day.

Another B vitamin I gave her was Inositol (B8). Inositol is believed to help stimulate the body in the production of serotonin and dopamine. It is also thought to help fight against damaging free radicals in the brain and other parts of the body. I started with ¼ teaspoon (600mg) once a day for two weeks and then went up to 1200mg every other day for two weeks. I did this for one month. After that, I began to give 600mg twice a week, on Mondays and Thursdays.

I also gave my wife Brewer's Yeast. Brewer's yeast contains minerals such as selenium and chromium and contains many complex B vitamins like B1 (thiamine), B2 (riboflavin), B3 (niacin), B5 (pantothenic acid), B6 (pyridoxine), B7 (biotin), B9 (folic acid), and many, many amino acids. I gave her one tablespoon a day. Brewer's yeast is believed to help support the nervous system as well as help support and maintain muscles used for digestion. The recommended dose is two tablespoons; however, the taste is very bitter. You can purchase the de-bittered form, but I prefer the supplement in its purest form.

I purchased a raw whole food multi-vitamin along with two powdered plant herbs, Maca root, and Ashwagandha. I gave my wife Maca root powder for its belief to help with menopause symptoms and its ability to nourish the endocrine and nervous system. Maca has high levels of iron and iodine which help promote healthy thyroid function as well as potassium, which helps muscle contraction and supports normal blood pressure levels. I gave her Ashwagandha powder for it's believed to help with relieving stress and anxiety and boosting brain function and memory. All of these supplements were mixed into a chocolate protein shake. I mixed them with un-sweetened Flaxseed milk or Oat Milk along with one or two bananas. I purchased a coffee bean grinder and used that to grind up the pills that were not in a powder capsule.

After a couple of months, I had to stop giving Crystal the CBD oil during this process. It was interfering with and disrupting her liver's ability to metabolize the medication. The liver's ability to metabolize drugs is called Cytochrome P450 (CYP450) and the CBD oil was interfering with the benefits Olanzapine was having on reducing her visual, auditory, and command hallucinations.

I should also mention that Crystal was on Zoloft, Ambien, Risperidone, and Seroquel during this time. (Not all at once). None of these medications worked. She suffered terrible side effects of worsening depression, aggression, hallucinations, insomnia, and anxiety with these as well. I was able to rule out the medications that were not working and keep her on the only medicine she is currently taking, Olanzapine, and request that her dose be increased at night from 5mg to 10mg along with the 2.5mg she was taking three times a day.

During this time, when I became a "Hood scientist," our psychologist, Dr. Marchita Masters, recommended that I get my wife into an I.O.P (Individualized Outpatient Program) to continue her treatment outside of the hospital.

I found a place here in Fresno, California called Sierra Meadows Behavioral Health. They have a program that helps people struggling with depression, anxiety, PTSD, bipolar, and other mental health disorders. I contacted our insurance for approval and then made an appointment to speak with the intake person at Sierra Meadows. I got my wife signed up; however, it was not easy to get her to go but I eventually convinced her to try. She went to this facility from Monday through Thursday for 3 hours a day. She participated in group therapy as well as many other modalities the facility had to offer. In addition to group therapy, she had individual therapy once a week, face-to-face with her therapist. Crystal struggled with group therapy at first. She has never been the one to talk about her feelings, especially in front of other people, but she slowly began to open up and speak about a few of the things she struggled with. She was enrolled in this program from February 2020 through August 2020. I would testify finally that Crystal's case never remained the same again. Her mind and body began to heal. I give all the glory to God for his grace, love, mercy, wisdom, and intervention.

I also want to thank the C.E.O of Sierra Meadows Behavioral Health Dr. Mathew Tatum for all of his help and support. I would also like to thank my wife's therapist Emily Gomez along with Dylan Vane, the therapist who conducted many of the group sessions that my wife participated in.

We never stopped seeing our psychologists- Dr. Marchita Masters and Dr. Kelly Horton. We are still under their care to this day. Their love and support have been both irreplaceable and invaluable. I would like to extend a very special, heart-filled thank you to Dr. Masters. During my quest to seek medical care for my wife, Dr. Masters' degree of understanding, dedication, and relentless compassion far exceeded any level of care I would expect to have received from any health care practitioner.

We reconnected in our relationship with God. We love and thank him for watching over us during this difficult journey.

On June 1st, 2020, my wife and I were evicted from our condo due to a sale by the owner.

On June 3rd, 2020, I was laid off from my place of employment.

In August of 2020, I was diagnosed with Depression and PTSD.

I look back on my life. I look back on my childhood. I look back on the things that I had done and the person that I had become. I look back on everything that I put my wife through and everything that we just went through. Although we are still a work in progress, this is what I realize.

It is clear to me. God sent my wife to me; it was not an accident that we met. It was not an accident how we met. It was no accident that we stayed together. Crystal was sent to me at a crucial time in my life. God sent her, knowing that I would need her love along with her strength. God gave her the power to love me enough to spark a change in my behavior. In making this change, I was able to be present for my wife, my best friend, during her time of need.

My childhood was horrible. It molded and shaped my negative thoughts and behavior for the first part of my existence. However, it also gave me resilience, perseverance, and patience. These very attributes would strengthen and return later in life to help me love my wife through her struggle with her mental illness.

You can change. You are not what you have been through. You are not the people that abused you. You are not worthless. Find someone to talk to: a family member, a friend, a therapist, a psychologist, or a psychiatrist. Start with self-love. If you feel that you are all alone or you feel like no one loves you...I love you... whomever you are and wherever you may be... we love you.

With brotherly love from our creator,

James and Crystal Bass

AFTERWORD
THE ILLUSTRATIVE AND ILLUMINATING
CASE OF CRYSTAL AND JAMES

O n November 2, 2019, there were two back-to-back online telehealth appointments on my schedule for Crystal Bass, whom I had never met. I received a notification that my new patient had entered the telehealth waiting room, so I logged onto my laptop. To my surprise, her husband, James appeared instead. There was dim lighting in the room. He spoke in a low voice and appeared to be very concerned and somewhat anxious. He periodically looked around as if someone might walk in as he provided information regarding Crystal's behavioral health issues and his attempts to care for her.

James spoke almost the entire first session until I asked if I would see his wife. I met with Crystal for the last 15 minutes of the first session. I initially thought they looked alike because they both had caramel-colored skin and were both very attractive. Crystal was kind with soft eyes and a warm face. She was relieved that I was Black; this helped her feel more at ease. James was there to get us started on the second session and he left us alone after that. I was impressed with James's attention to detail, the love and tenderness he exuded, and how involved he was in his wife's care. This was my introduction to Crystal and James Bass and an excellent representation of the next three years of my work with them. On December 18, 2019, James also became my patient to address caretaker stress and unresolved childhood abuse issues.

This couple is truly inspiring and the epitome of strength and perseverance. The saying "going through hell and back" doesn't begin to describe their individual and collective journeys. They both got through their torturous childhoods which included unfathomable abuses by parents and their partners. They managed to get through the fear and trauma of domestic violence early in their relationship. As their lives settled and they seemed to be on a positive path, Crystal entered City College and the experience there violently ripped the Band-Aid off her unhealed emotional wounds. It unleashed an avalanche of trauma and sheer terror for both that eclipsed previous traumatic experiences. That was when James brought her to me, and our journey together began.

Crystal is gorgeous and a truly amazing woman. She overcame a childhood full of terrible abuse and neglect to become a successful entrepreneur. She owned a daycare center and also took care of foster kids. She fully opened her home and her heart. She showered each child with unconditional love, the exact thing that wasn't afforded to her as a child. On some level, pouring love into each child helped her own inner child. She is a fighter; there is no quit in her. Crystal needed every ounce of her courage to cope with her illness, which she did with James' steadfastness and undying love. This is the reason I was shocked when Crystal told me one day that James abused her in the past. It was hard for me to believe that the man who I had come to know as being completely devoted to Crystal was previously her abuser.

James had a full-time job where he excelled even in the face of an excessively high level of work-related stress. He was also Crystal's caretaker; they had no one else to depend on. James was a loving husband who did whatever he had to do to ensure Crystal got the care she needed. He admitted to me one day that he did abuse her early in their relationship. When talking about it, he was overwhelmed with grief while acknowledging how he added to Crystal's trauma. He described how and why he made the 360-degree change. The fact that James went from violently abused child to wife abuser is not surprising. The fact that he went from wife abuser to wife protector and caretaker, with as much gentleness, love, and patience as any person can exhibit, is what is surprising to me.

The Bass' story is one of resilience, fortitude, love, inspiration, and forgiveness. James became obsessed with learning everything about Crystal's diagnoses, treatments, and medications. He did extensive research. He read everything he could and took copious notes regarding her symptoms and how each new medication impacted her functioning. He became so adept at managing her medications that he was able to advise her various psychiatrists on which medications were best for her. There were times, based on his research and observations, he made effective unilateral decisions to remove certain medications and add supplements instead. Although it's important to be actively involved in one's care, I would advise against anyone adjusting their medication regimen without their doctor's prior approval. Even so, the changes James made had a dramatic and positive impact on Crystal's quality of life. I stood and still stand in amazement. In fact,

I am requesting that an accredited medical school consider awarding James Bass an honorary medical degree. All the prospective schools need to do is review his in-depth documentation based on research, observations, and analyses and they would likely agree.

The situation with Crystal and James illuminates many issues:

1) All child abuse is horrible and should never happen under any circumstances! It has an extremely detrimental long-term impact on a child's development, and future relationships with self and others and can lead to behavioral health issues.

2) People can change. James went from being an abuser to a loving husband once he came to terms with the fact that he was repeating the cycle. He realized he didn't want to be like his abusers any longer.

3) As a society, we need to have a robust, honest, and ongoing conversation about behavioral health issues. We get close now and then when a celebrity commits suicide. We are shocked and saddened and then go back to our willful denial. Most people who attempt suicide don't want to die, they just want the emotional pain to stop, and they don't know how to make it stop. If you or anyone you know is contemplating suicide, dial 988 which is the new number for the National Suicide Prevention Lifeline.

4) There are far too many people suffering in silence because of the myths that exist in society. People don't want to be labeled crazy or weak; they don't want a "shrink" telling them what to do. This is not what behavioral health treatment is.

5) With love, support and perseverance, people can overcome a harsh beginning to life and seemingly insurmountable obstacles in life.

Crystal and James can attest to the fact that therapy is a vehicle to help one become a better version of themselves, resolve past trauma, improve relationships, learn new coping strategies, improve communication skills, forgive oneself, and improve self-esteem. Not every therapist is right for every client, just like not all shoes are right for all feet. If you get a therapist that doesn't fit, please keep trying. When you find the therapist that fits your situation and interaction style, you will have the opportunity of benefiting in a way you never thought possible.

I propose that therapy or counseling should be like regular physical checkups. Adults and kids can see a therapist periodically to determine if there's something there that needs attention. Kids get yearly physicals and go to the dentist twice per year just to make sure they are developing properly. Girls of a certain age get yearly pap smears. Women get regular mammograms. Men get prostate screenings. Adults get colonoscopies. We should think of therapy the same way, and this will help to remove the stigma.

Again, if you or anyone you know is considering suicide, dial 988 to be connected to the National Suicide Prevention Lifeline. Another great resource is National Alliance on Mental Illness (nami.org). If you are struggling in your life for any reason, go get help! Going to a therapist can be the best thing you ever did for yourself. Just ask Crystal and James.

Dr. Marchita Masters

Pediatric, Adult, and Family Psychologist

www.ingramcontent.com/pod-product-compliance
Lightning Source LLC
Chambersburg PA
CBHW071444090426
42737CB00011B/1772